The Last Waterman

A True Story

"What really bothers me is that a man soon won't be able to make his way on the Bay, no matter how hard he works. The water just doesn't have much life left in it. You asked me what's the worst problem on the Bay. That's it, no life in the water."

The Last Waterman

Crisfield Publishing Company
Crisfield, Maryland

Typeset by

Fred Brown
102 Carmichael Court
Cary, NC 27511

Printed in the United States of America

ISBN 0-9620439-0-7

Table of Contents

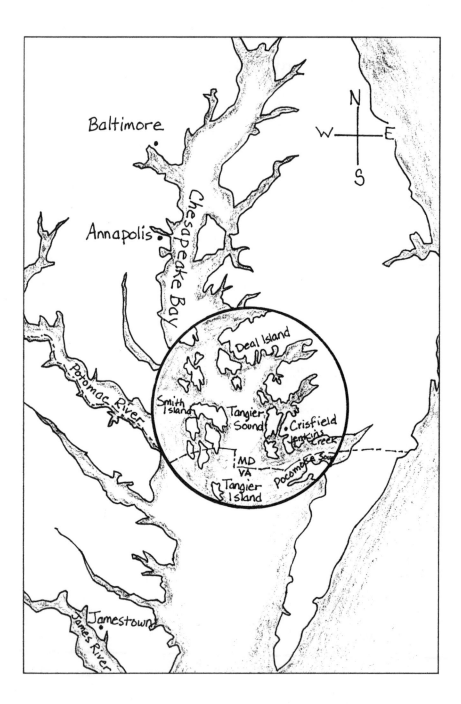

Chesapeake Bay with Tangier Sound magnified
(Illustration by Nancy Kramer)

Illustrations

by Becky Lowe
Maritime artist
Crisfield, Maryland

The shanty at Jenkins Creek

Chapter 1
Jenkins Creek

Jenkins Creek was quiet, not a soul in sight. The long, rickety wharf stretched out in front of me across a hundred yards of boggy marsh and another fifty yards of water before it reached the weathering shanty, perched precariously on spindly pilings near the middle of the creek. Tied up beside the shanty, at the very end of the wharf where the water stood the deepest, was the old boat. It all looked very much the way I remembered it.

A blanket of gray clouds scudded overhead and gusts of wind rattled the dry marsh grass around me as I picked my way along the wharf, hurrying as much as I dared while still being careful not to step on any boards that were cracked or suspiciously bowed. I turned up the collar of my jacket to protect myself from the trailing breeze. After thirty years in an office, I had forgotten how a northeaster could chill you to the bone out here on the edge of the Bay, even before October begins. I wondered how much more I had forgotten.

I merely glanced at the boat as I hurried past it, eager to get to the other side of the shanty where I would be protected from the cutting wind. I rounded the corner and there, sheltered from the breeze, sitting on an old crate with a clutter of ropes and buoys around his feet and a stack of salt stained baskets beside him, I found a lone, burley figure in a plaid flannel shirt absent mindedly staring out across the choppy waves toward the wide mouth of the creek.

"Hi, Hon," I said.

He peered over his shoulder at me.

1

"I didn't know you were home," he said. I had hoped he would be happy to see me, but his voice showed no particular enthusiasm.

"Home?" I responded. "This isn't home to me anymore."

"I suppose it isn't," he said. "You move around more than a gypsy."

"They told me you were getting the boat ready for oystering," I said, to change the subject. "I figured you might need some help."

"Naw," he grumbled. "I put up the mast by myself. That's the hardest part."

That's Hon, rarely asking for help, rarely admitting that he can't do whatever he tries his hand at.

"Looks to me like you still have a long way to go to get ready."

"I'm not goin' oysterin'."

Not going oystering! How can that be? Hon spent every winter oystering, just as Floyd had done before his illness forced him ashore.

"What are you going to do?"

"I've decided to go back to the shipyard this winter. I welded for 'em a couple of years ago when the Bay froze over. When spring came and I quit to go crabbin', they told me they'd have a job for me any time I wanted it. I'm goin' to take 'em up on their offer."

"Why did you put up your mast, then?"

"Habit, I suppose. Been doin' it every year, but the longer I worked at it, the more I thought about how miserable it's goin' to be out there on the water. When the wind's a blowin' out of the north and your teeth are chatterin' and your hands are all cracked open from the cold and you're not catchin' enough oysters to make any money, it's mighty hard to enjoy what you're doin'."

He glanced at his watch. "Hate to be unsociable," he said as he rose to his feet, "but it's time for me to go ashore. I got a meetin' tonight. Did you walk down here?"

"Yeah, I needed to stretch my legs after the drive."

"Might as well ride back with me," he said.

Knowing how cold I would be walking to the house facing that wind, I nodded my agreement.

"Follow me," he said. "I know where the good boards are."

As I traced my brother's footsteps along the weathered walkway across the marsh, I could not help but compare what the two of us had become. A little over six feet tall and weighing about two hundred thirty pounds, he appeared to be a typical example of a rugged Chesapeake waterman. His rolling gait carried a bit of a swagger, one that I sensed not as a show of bravado, but as an indication that he cared not one hoot about the combined opinions of all the rest of the world. With his thick hands and massive forearms protruding from his rolled up flannel sleeves, he seemed oblivious to the chilling breeze. His heavy denim jeans were stained with grease, and the back of his shirt was smeared with mud.

When we were growing up on this creek, I had been bigger and stronger than him. But now I watched my diet and practiced a daily exercise regimen to keep my weight near one-seventy, because any more than that aggravated my chronic back problem. My office and my house and my car were all air conditioned, so I no longer adjusted well to changes in temperature, and I couldn't think of a single piece of clothing I owned that carried a grease stain.

We climbed into his old Dodge pickup truck and rattled the short distance up the road to his house. He pulled into the edge of his yard and parked beside a stack of rusty crab pots.

"See ya later," he said.

"Yeah," I replied. "I'll be around a couple of days."

I walked across the road, followed the path that led between the apple trees and the garden, and stepped up onto the back porch of my parents' neat, two story house. As I opened the door, I glanced out back. Marsh, nothing but a treeless, salt water marsh stretched to the horizon. They seemed to live at the very edge of civilization, fitting for the way my father had earned his income.

My mother and my wife, Virginia, were busy loading the table. There were bowls of string beans and pickled beets, a basket full of hot biscuits, a dish of butter and a jar of fig preserves, and a huge platter piled high with fried soft crabs. Even though Floyd and Margaret were retired and living on a very limited income, I couldn't imagine a meal better than this on anybody's table. Except for the biscuits and the butter, it all came from either the garden or the Bay.

As we ate, our conversation bounced around from one topic to another, like the weather and the church and the depressed economy of the town, and then it settled on Hon.

"He's not making any money on the water," Margaret said. "I don't understand the whole situation, but I know he doesn't work like your father used to. Floyd went out every day, whether it was fit or not."

"That I did," Floyd said between forkfuls of crab, "every day. Sometimes I worked when the boat was bouncin' so hard I could barely stand up. But I worked anyway, and I always caught oysters, plenty of 'em. That Bay's full of oysters, if you just know where to look. Always has been, always will be.

Anybody with a boat can make a good livin' at oysterin' if he wants to work at it."

I could tell they were not pleased with the way the family seafood business had been going since Hon began running it. Profits never were good, but Floyd generally had a little money left over at the end of the year. Now there wasn't even enough coming in to keep the shanty in good repair. They felt one of the problems was that Hon spent too much time during the winter at things other than oystering.

We had just finished our dessert of baked apples when we heard Hon's wife, Yvonne, come in the side door. We moved to the family room where we could sit around and talk.

"Hon says he'll be welding this winter," I said. "I'm glad to see he's finally thinking about leaving the water."

"It's not that he wants to," Yvonne replied. "Looks like this is going to be a bad winter. Last week I pulled samples of oysters, and they're mighty scarce."

I knew she worked for the state health department, running all around the central part of the Bay in a small boat collecting samples of water for analysis, but I didn't know she also sampled oysters.

"Why do you sample oysters?" I asked.

"We do that every year, just before the season begins, to check for contamination. I have a little dredge that I pull behind the boat. I'll drag it over an oyster rock to pick up a few, put them in a sack with a tag showing where I found them, then go to another rock. Most of what I pulled up this year were what Hon calls 'boxes', empty shells still hinged together with no oyster inside. You know they just recently died because the shells haven't come apart yet."

"What's causing them to die?"

"We don't know. And we won't know how many live

5

ones are left until the season opens and the watermen start working. If any are out there, they'll find them. But I sure didn't find many. Hon hates to admit it, but he probably won't be able to make a living on the water this winter."

"He said he has a meeting tonight."

"He's speaking at a public hearing."

Hon, speaking! I could not imagine him standing before a crowd.

"Since he was elected president of the county watermen's association," Yvonne continued, "he often gets called on to represent them. This meeting is about some proposed environmental regulation."

I was sure I knew how he stood on that issue, for watermen have always opposed any regulation. As long as there have been watermen, they have always believed they had a God given right to anything that flew or swam or laid on the bottom of the Bay, and that no human authority was justified in depriving them of that right.

The talk soon turned to knitting and Christmas and how quiet it was around the house since the children were grown and on their own, so I slipped upstairs to the bedroom. I raised the south window a bit so I could smell the saltiness of the air and hear the croaks and the calls of the night loving marsh creatures. I turned off the light and stretched out on the bed. As I lay there in the darkness, my mind traveled back across the years to when Hon and I had chosen our separate paths.

We had grown up here on the creek together, playing around the shanty and in the skiffs. Then we each left to serve in the military. Hon joined the Marines, I was drafted a few months later. After my military duty ended, I completed college and then took a job working with a computer company. I had not been back very often since then, but my current assignment brought me close enough so I could drive in for a weekend. That is, I could if nothing demanded that I be at the office.

Hon went off to engineering school when he returned from the Marines, but shortly after he graduated he came back to these crumbling wharves and old wooden boats. As intelligent and talented as he was, I often wondered why he had not chosen to do something more worthwhile with his life. To me, he seemed driven to waste it away, spending each summer fishing his crab pots and each winter probing the cold Bay for oysters. If a man could do anything else for a living, I did not understand why he would want to be a waterman, spending half of his life trying to keep the boat running and the other half out on the Bay in all kinds of weather trying to catch enough crabs and oysters to pay his bills.

But being a waterman isn't like having an ordinary job. It's more like being possessed by a passion that gains such control over you that you willingly follow it, no matter what. For a man to continue to survive on the water, he needs to have something special bred into him, just like the migrating instincts are bred into a wild goose. When a man has these special instincts, he just naturally tends to spend most of his daylight hours on the water, and many of his night hours, as well. He only feels at home on the deck of a rolling boat, solid ground seems alien to him. He schedules his life by the tides rather than by the clock. He reads the current events that are important to him from the waters of the Bay, and from the sky above it and the marshes beside it, just as drylanders read a newspaper.

Some people come from the city and spend a couple of days here on the Bay, maybe even a couple of weeks, then go back and write an article for a magazine telling everybody what it's like to be a waterman, but they don't know. Others even buy a boat and work it a year or two. They think they are watermen, but pretty soon the glamor wears thin and the boat is for sale.

Those who stick with being a waterman are the ones who are born into it, or at least have the instincts. Hon and I were both born into it. He also had the instincts.

Outsiders never come to realize that a waterman is not like them. He is more like an untamed creature, a part of the pattern of life on the Bay where all exist by preying on others. The fittest survive for a while, the weak do not. As time passes and the hazards of this way of life continue to come as a flood, all of the Bay creatures eventually succumb to either the laws of probability or the disabling effects of the aging process. Floyd beat the laws of probability, he survived and stayed on the water until he was just short of seventy years old. Hon may not be able to hang on anywhere near that long.

But why should I be concerned about Hon? I had enough of my own problems to think about, I didn't need to bother myself with his. Besides, the drive to Crisfield had been long and tiring, and I felt myself drifting off to sleep.

"Hey, you goin' to stay in bed all day?"

I raised up and squinted through the window screen. I could only see a shadow in the blackness outside, but I knew that booming voice had to belong to Hon.

"What time is it?"

"Time for breakfast. I got a lot to do today, thought you might want to go along."

I felt around in the dark to find my clothes without waking Virginia, then I fumbled my way out of the bedroom and turned on the light over the once familiar stairway to make sure I didn't start the day by diving head first into the hall below. As I stepped out of the house and closed the door behind me, I glanced eastward. A very faint gray glow on the horizon hinted that a sunrise was on the way.

The Circle Inn was crowded with sun bronzed men wearing flannel jackets and grease blackened pants. They were the watermen from Crisfield and Apes Hole and countless nearby creeks who stopped there for breakfast on mornings when they weren't out early in their boats. The ones who had been forced ashore also dropped in to see if the catch was improving, if maybe they could leave their tiresome land bound jobs and go back to oystering. The talk was all dismal. Two men at a table near the kitchen door announced that they had decided to hang up their tongs and look for jobs come Monday morning. Several others were undecided about whether they would continue.

As we climbed into the pickup to leave, Hon said, "Well, there's goin' to be less men to divide those few oysters among this year. I hate to see them have to quit, but every man who leaves the water puts that much more money into the pockets of the ones who stay. There are only so many marketable oysters in the Bay this year, and we're going to catch just about every one."

Catch every oyster in the Bay—unthinkable, and I told him so.

"Not like it used to be," he replied as he pulled out of the parking lot. "Back when we were boys a man could be a hog if he wanted, work seven days a week, rain or sleet or gale, and he could always bring in a load of oysters. Not any more. A man's not going to catch many oysters any day now. If he has any sense, he only goes out in decent weather so he doesn't

9

stand as great a chance of damagin' his equipment or gettin' drowned."

Drowning, you don't hear watermen talk about that often, but it is one of the ever present dangers of oystering in the deep water. One of our neighborhood buddies drowned while oystering, and when a tragedy hits that close, it never totally leaves your mind.

"Trouble is," he continued, "we still have a lot of hogs out there, men who want their share of the oysters and everybody else's too. That's one of the problems on the Bay, but it's not the worst one."

I asked what the worst problem was, but he gave no indication of having heard my question. He had always been that way. Ask him any question you want, he'll answer the ones he wants, when he's ready.

Hon pulled off the road and parked right at the end of the shanty wharf. Seems no matter where he starts out to go, he always ends up at the shanty, beside the boat. We had only walked a couple of steps along the wharf when he stopped and peered down at the marsh.

"Want to see somethin' interestin'?" he asked.

Before I could reply he kneeled down and brushed away a pile of dried grass and trash, revealing a massive slab of weathered wood that had washed up against the pilings.

"You know what that is? That's the side of an old log canoe, the last one on this creek."

I kneeled beside him for a closer look. I had heard the old timers tell of their log canoes, but I had never seen one. The slab was about twenty feet long, nearly two inches thick, gently curved, and tapered toward the end that was visible above the mud and matted grass. I marveled at the thought of a man carving a boat this big from a tree trunk with simple hand tools.

Hon reached down and pointed to a neat, round hole in the log about the diameter of a pencil.

"That's a depth gauge," he said. "They carved the outside of the canoe first. After they got it to where it looked like a boat, they bored rows of holes in it. They chipped away on the inside 'till they came to the holes, and they knew they had the right thickness. Then they drove wooden plugs into the holes. With all your education, can you think of a better way than that?"

I was amazed at how much he seemed to know about the ways of the watermen from generations past. I had imagined that he was too busy trying to make a living to consider the practices of years ago.

"Don't mean to belittle education," he said as he stood up. "We just need to realize that those people had their own kind of education. They couldn't go to the store and buy whatever they needed, they generally had to catch it or make it with their own hands. If we were thrown into their circumstances, most of us would starve to death before we could learn what they knew."

That thought had occasionally entered my mind. If our food distribution system were to break down for some reason and our supermarkets closed their doors, Virginia and I would probably go hungry within a week, but Hon wouldn't. He practiced the art of survival every day.

We left the canoe behind and walked on toward the shanty. I mentioned to him that Yvonne had said oysters were scarce.

"That's no secret. You should have figured it out by yourself."

"How?"

"Look around. Tell me what you see."

I looked around, but I saw nothing to give me a clue. The only movement on the creek was the ripple of the water and the slight tug of his boat against its lines. The only sound was the wind occasionally rattling the pulley at the top of the mast.

"I don't see anything."

"Doesn't that seem unusual? Oyster season opens next week. Have you forgotten how the creek used to be at this time of the year?"

I had forgotten, until he mentioned it. Now, a vivid picture from the past sprang to my mind, a vision of half a hundred men scrambling around on their boats, busy with their last minute preparations. It was a joyful scene I recalled, some of the men singing their Methodist hymns as they hammered away, others shouting back and forth across the water and joking as they patched and painted the scars left over from the summer's work, each of them happy about the prospect of soon being out on the Bay again, plunging their long shafted tongs into the water and pulling them up, hand over hand, and dumping the oysters into the hold until, by the end of the day, the pile would be waist deep. Sometimes I believed the men enjoyed catching the oysters more than they enjoyed spending the money they gained from it.

"Where do all the other tongers keep their boats?"

"There aren't any others, not on this creek anyway, and I really don't know why I'm still here. I barely made enough this past year to keep food on the table and fuel in the boat, but it's still hard to give up."

"I'm sorry, Hon, I...."

"That's all right, Glenn. I'm not lookin' for sympathy, it's my own choosin'. I've done what I wanted, workin' on the Bay, and I've enjoyed every day of it. But right now I feel like a man I saw on television the other night, standin' and watchin' his farm bein' auctioned off. He'd spent his entire life there, but it was bein' taken away from him and he was helpless to do anything about it. Well, I'm as helpless as him. The Bay is bein' taken away, too, and I can't do a thing to prevent it. No need to cry, though. I'm just goin' to have to find a job ashore, and I'm sure I can, even though I am forty-six years old. I can weld on those barges at the shipyard, or I can drive a truck, or I can do somethin' else if neither of those works out. Where I find a job isn't what bothers me, I'll adjust."

He restlessly paced the wharf beside his boat. To consider leaving the water, this was a traumatic decision for him. I had learned to jump from one job to another without any remorse when a good opportunity presented itself, but for him to think about going ashore was unbearable. To admit failure, to surrender his independence, Hon couldn't easily do that. His nature would not allow it.

He stopped his pacing. "What really bothers me," he said, "is that a man soon won't be able to make his way on the Bay, no matter how hard he works. The water just doesn't have much life left in it. You asked me what's the worst problem on the Bay. That's it, no life in the water."

He took his glasses off and wiped them on his shirt tail.

"Our family," he said, "has made a livin' on this Bay for as long as anybody. Eleven generations we've worked the water, eight of them from this same creek."

I noticed a glistening in his eyes before he put his glasses back on and turned away from me.

"Do you realize that I'm the only one in the family left?" he said as he looked out toward the Bay.

"I'm the last waterman."

Chapter 2
A Time of Gathering

Our next trip to Crisfield was for a reason other than to visit my parents. I had written a book about two very popular wildfowl artists, Lem and Steve Ward, and it was being introduced at the Easton Waterfowl Festival, one of the most prominent shows in the country for wildfowl art enthusiasts. I had agreed to appear at Easton Friday and Saturday to autograph copies. Virginia and I drove to Crisfield Thursday afternoon. From there, I could easily reach Easton by the time the festival opened the following day.

Virginia enjoyed going to Crisfield, but she was not looking forward to sitting for two days in a booth behind a stack of books, so she suggested I ask Hon if he would like to make the trip to Easton with me.

That sounded like a good idea. I walked across the road and knocked on his door.

"I'm down here."

He sounded like he must be under the house. I walked around to the south side, in the direction of his voice, and found a couple of panels pulled away from the foundation.

"Stick your head under here. I want you to see somethin'."

I kneeled on one of the panels, trying not to muddy my pants, and peered under the house. Hon was flat on his belly in the dirt.

"Look at the way this house was put together, every joint is mortised. See how that sill is notched and the floor joist is cut to fit perfectly into it. Houses just aren't built like that nowadays."

"That is interesting, but you didn't crawl under there just to find out how it was put together, did you?"

"Naw," he said as he wiggled out of the opening. "The kitchen floor is saggin' and I wanted to see why. The problem is the foundation has settled a bit, but I guess that's to be expected. This house is two hundred years old. I traced it back at the court house. That's a fine way to spend a rainy day, goin' through those old records."

"Would you like to go to the Waterfowl Festival tomorrow?"

"Sure," he replied as he brushed the dirt off the front of his shirt. "I'm barely catchin' enough oysters to pay my boat expenses. If I'm not goin' to make any money anyway, I might as well do it where I can be warm and dry."

"You told me you were going to quit oystering."

"I decided to stick with it one more season," he said. "Don't ask me why, because I certainly did it against my better judgement.

"Time to go to the shanty," he continued. "The boat leaks right much, being forty years old. Even when I'm not usin' it, I have to check to make sure the pump is workin'. Want to come along?"

"Sure," I replied, and I followed him to his truck.

As we neared the boat, we could see it was sitting high in the water. This was proof enough the pump was working. Hon could have seen that by driving a little farther along the road, and would not have needed to walk down the long wharf. I knew, though, that he didn't come here just to look. He was a waterman, and he had to spend at least a part of each day on the boat. Floyd had been that way, and so had our grandfather before him.

15

Hon stepped down off the wharf onto the boat, opened the cover over the engine, and checked the oil. He then walked back to the controls, pumped the gas, and turned the starter key. The motor groaned once, then coughed and caught with a roar. A blast of black smoke shot out from each exhaust pipe, and the whole boat twitched to life, shaking all over as though it anticipated a run out to the Bay. Strange, I thought, how I attributed human characteristics to a boat, especially to a big, wooden boat. I supposed I had learned that as a child growing up in a waterman's home. There, the boat was always treated, and even spoken of, like it was another member of the family. A very important member of the family, at that.

Hon slowed the engine to an idle and puttered around a bit, rearranging his ropes to make sure they had not become tangled. Then he turned off the ignition switch and stepped up onto the wharf.

"I imagine we'll be gettin' back late tomorrow," he said. "She'll be all right 'til then."

He pointed toward the mouth of the creek, out to where it widened and met the open waters.

"You ever try to imagine," he asked, "how this Bay looked when the first English settlers arrived?"

"No, I keep my mind too busy for dreaming."

"That's too bad, every man needs a dream. When I'm out there on the water by myself," he continued, "I think a lot about how our family ended up on this creek, and what they found here, and how they managed to survive. Then, when the weather turns too bad to go out, I'll stop by the library and read anything I can find that helps me to learn more about our history. Aren't you interested in our history?"

"Well, yeah. I guess so."

"I can see you're runnin' over with enthusiasm," he said.

"Surely you know that our family traces back to the first English settlers at Jamestown."

I knew our family legend concerning Thomas Lawson, that he was a construction engineer and a leader at the first colony when it was established. This was a nice story, the kind people tell while sitting around a fire on a cold winter night, but I doubted its authenticity.

"Let me tell you my version of the colonial history of the Chesapeake Bay, and how we came to live on this creek," he said as he sat down on a crate, leaned back against the weathered side of the shanty, and clasped his hands together across his broad chest.

He began with the motives for establishing the colony. The advertised motives were to expand His Majesty's empire, to extend the Christian faith, and to gain a profit. John Smith, who had already earned a reputation as an adventurer in Europe, was selected as the leader.

The colonists were expecting food to be plentiful here, and it was, for the waters of the Bay were full of fish and oysters. They managed quite well during the summer, when they could wade out into the shallows and haul fish ashore in their nets. They ate as much as they wanted, then tossed the remainder aside to rot. When winter came, they were unprepared for its severity. The fish moved out to deeper water, leaving them little to eat. They rationed their meager stores of peas and corn, they foraged in the fields, and they picked up oysters along the shoreline. Most of them starved to death. A few survived by imitating the ways of the Indians. Thomas Lawson was one of the survivors.

The Virginia colony did not make the profit that was expected, so King Charles I granted to Lord Calvert the right to establish another colony, named Maryland, on the shores of the upper part of the Chesapeake Bay. The king promised Calvert all the land on the western side of the Bay north of the Potomac River, and the entire peninsula on the eastern side of the Bay. The owners of the Virginia Company, which held the charter for the struggling colony, objected strenuously. They argued that they had a considerable investment in the entire Bay and the land around it.

The king reconsidered, and let the Virginia Company keep the southern part of the peninsula because they had settled several towns there. In 1632, the king officially approved the boundary between the two colonies. It was to run along the southern shoreline of the Potomac River to an Indian village named Cinquach, just south of where the Potomac flowed into the Bay. From there, the line was to run straight across the Bay to a place called Watkins Point, and from there eastward to the Atlantic Ocean. This gave Maryland all of the Potomac River and all of the Bay area north of Cinquach, including one trading settlement that Virginia had established on Kent Island.

The Virginians resented the Maryland intrusion into what they considered to be their Bay. William Claiborne, the leader of the Kent Island trading settlement, was particularly adamant. He fitted a sailing vessel with cannons and set out to attack the offenders. The governor of the Maryland colony responded by dispatching an armed sloop from St. Mary's City. The tiny, improvised warships met at the mouth of the Pocomoke River, near the Eastern Shore. After the cannon fire ended and the smoke of the battle cleared, the Maryland ship had prevailed.

The Maryland militia eventually subdued Claiborne, and gained uncontested control of the upper part of the Bay. The boundary, however, remained a matter for dispute. Virginia and Maryland agreed that the line came ashore on the eastern side of the Bay at Watkins Point, for that was clearly documented by the king when he granted the Maryland charter. But they did not agree where Watkins Point was located.

Maryland claimed that Watkins Point was on the Pocomoke Sound, almost directly eastward across the Bay from the known boundary line along the southern bank of the Potomac. Virginia claimed this point was on the Nanticoke River, much farther to the north. To strengthen its claim, Maryland hurried to survey the land along the northern shore of the Pocomoke and patent it to farmers, who were required to pledge their allegiance to the colony of Maryland and agree to immediately settle on the property.

A few years after these first farmers settled, Charles Calvert of Maryland and Governor Scarborough of Virginia agreed on the location of the boundary line, running it between Tangier Island and Smith Island, and bringing it ashore at a point of land on the northern side of the Pocomoke. About eighty years later, Hance Lawson sailed northward from Virginia and settled just above this line, on a strip of land between the Pocomoke Sound and the Little Annemessex River that was known as Annemessex Neck. There, he built his house near the head of Jenkins Creek.

Hon pointed toward the head of the creek, where the bridge crossed over it.

"None of the towns and roads we're so used to were here back then," he said. "A few cart trails led from the tobacco farms to the nearest harbor. The water was the colonial highway, everything moved by boat. People traveled by boat, tobacco and lumber were shipped out by boat, tools and housewares and cattle were shipped in by boat. Everybody lived close to the water, everybody depended on it one way or another."

"I guess just about all of the people here were farmers at the time Hance arrived," I said.

"I doubt that," Hon replied. "Timber was important, too. Annemessex is an Indian word that means place where big trees grow beside the water, so we know there was plenty of big timber here then, even though we don't have any now. A lot of other tradesmen lived here too, hirin' out to the farmers and the timber cutters. There would have been barrel makers and teamsters and schooner captains and, of course, you know about the picaroons."

"I've heard of them, but I don't know what they did."

"They were pirates," Hon said. "There were whole towns of 'em near here, places with names like Devil Island and Rogues Point and Damned Quarter. They just moved onto a piece of high land near the water and defied any attempt to impose authority over 'em. They were probably the original settlers around here, because they didn't need any surveys or approvals. They made their livin' by raidin' the shippin' in the Bay, and occasionally plunderin' the other settlements. This was a rough and lawless land back then."

"Why do you suppose Hance came here?"

"We can only guess what was on his mind, but we know he was a waterman and an unlicensed preacher, so we can be sure that he was independent by nature and didn't care at all for the Church of Virginia to tell him what to believe. He probably came here because Maryland offered greater religious freedom."

I picked up Hon early the next morning to begin the drive to Easton. He was more subdued than normal, maybe even a bit depressed. I asked what was troubling him.

"Last year," he said, "fewer oysters were caught in the Bay than any other year since the state began keepin' records."

"Why is that?" I asked, noting that any time his attention was not diverted by activity around him, he was thinking about the Bay or the plight of the watermen.

"They just aren't there to catch any more. Lots of people have theories, and most of 'em are pointin' to the waterman as the culprit. The Tidewater Fisheries scientists say we've caught up so many oysters there aren't enough left to reproduce and replace what we take each year. They're the state agency that has the responsibility for overseein' the seafood industry on the Bay, so they're the ones who propose new regulations to the legislature. They've banned catchin' shad and they've banned catchin' rockfish, and I'm afraid they're soon goin' to tighten up the restrictions on catchin' oysters. If they do, they'll restrict most of us right out of business. We used to depend on shad and rockfish for our springtime income, but now we have nothin' between the time we quit oysterin' and the time crabbin' begins in May. Used to be a man could still be catchin' plenty of oysters when the season ended in the spring. The last couple of years we ran out of oysters about Christmas. I expect we'll be finished by Thanksgivin' this year, and that only gives us seven weeks of work. If our oyster catch drops off any more, because of either the supply or the restrictions, that will be the end of the independent Chesapeake waterman."

"Looks to me like you'll either have more restrictions or you're bound to have fewer oysters. One of those two seems inevitable."

"I'm afraid so," he abruptly responded, "but we're not the reason for the scarcity. I've said it before, and I'll say it again,

21

the problem is the water quality."

I thought back to a waterman I had known when I was a boy. He never caught many crabs, and he always blamed someone else. His problem was that he never modernized. He continued crabbing the same way he had when he was a boy, with just a small skiff and no motor. He claimed he wasn't catching enough crabs to support his growing family because the motor boats were poisoning the water. One day, another waterman started out of the creek and ran over something with his boat. He couldn't get his motor restarted, so he drifted into shallow water and climbed out to see what had happened. He found a rusty crab pot tangled around his propeller. Someone had filled the channel with old, abandoned crab pots. The watermen on the creek all knew who had done it, and swore they would burn the culprit's house down if he didn't clean out the channel. He and his son spent the remainder of the day dragging the old pots from the water and tossing them onto the bank, but he never changed his mind or his ways. The last time I saw him, he was still crabbing in his little skiff, and still complaining that the motor boats were poisoning the water.

Maybe Hon needed to change, maybe his techniques and his equipment had become outdated. Maybe all watermen had to change. I decided against suggesting this, though, for his previous response had been so emphatic and so final I was certain that as far as he was concerned the matter was closed.

As we neared Easton, he perked up.

"Glenn," he said, "I've decided what I need to do. I need to write a book."

"What about?" I asked.

"About the independent watermen on the Bay, and how their way of life is threatened. I know I'm not a scientist or a scholar, but *I am* a waterman."

"So the watermen will be the good guys in your book," I said. "You might have trouble convincing people of that, since so many think the watermen are the chief villains."

"But I have some very strong evidence, I'll even call it proof, to show that the watermen are not the problem."

"That's a rather bold claim. What's your proof?"

"The grass," he said. "You remember how the eel grass used to grow on the bottoms of the sounds and the rivers and the creeks. There was so much we all considered it a nuisance. Well, every strand is gone now, and nobody can blame us for catchin' too much of that. When the water quality is so poor the grass all dies, how can anyone expect the oysters and the shad and the rockfish to survive?"

The Waterfowl Festival was a big event. It coincided with the opening of the hunting season, and since Easton was at the center of the wintering grounds for the Canada goose, thousands of hunters were crowded into the small city. The business district had taken on the atmosphere of an oriental bazaar, the sidewalks all covered with exhibitors and the streets choked with people milling about. Hon and I took our positions at the booth assigned to me and spread out several copies of the book on the table.

Business was slow at first because our booth was away from the main crowd, so Hon struck up a conversation with the exhibitors sitting beside us. They were Bob and Alice Lippson, marine biologists who were selling and autographing their new book about plants and animals of the Chesapeake. Hon told them about the book he intended to write, and then began to relate some of his experiences on the water. Everything that happens to Hon seems hilarious, especially when he tells it. He soon had Bob laughing so hard the tears were streaming down his cheeks and he was forced to sit down because of the pain in his side. Hon kept on telling his stories until Bob finally asked him to go somewhere else until the pain subsided.

Hon took off to see the carving exhibits, leaving me alone at the booth. After Bob had recovered sufficiently to carry on a conversation, he and I began to discuss the book Hon had mentioned to him. When I stated that Hon was lacking the technical knowledge he would need to develop convincing arguments concerning the decline of sea life in the Bay, Bob surprised me by offering to help any way he could with the project.

"But," he cautioned as he handed me his business card, "be careful how much you listen to people like me. We researchers don't feel the same sense of urgency about the Bay that Hon does. This book needs to be about him, and other watermen like him. It needs to be their view of the Bay and its problems."

Hon returned after about an hour, leaned a chair back against the wall behind the booth, and watched as I discussed the book with any onlookers who showed an interest. But he couldn't stand the inactivity for long. He stepped up to the table and told me to take a seat and let him do the talking. He was certain he could sell more books than I could. My feet were tired so I was happy to do as he suggested, and pretty soon he had drawn a crowd. Since he was obviously better at attracting attention to the books than I was, I signed a stack of them and wandered off to see some of the other exhibits. When I came back I found that he had sold all the books I had signed, and was busy autographing them himself.

"Hey, Hon! You can't do that!"

"Sure I can. They wanted somebody to sign the books. I told 'em I was your brother, and that was good enough as far as they were concerned. Why should anyone else care?"

By the time the festival closed late that evening, we were both tired. We drove southward through miles of dark farmland and crossed the Choptank River bridge before we found a restaurant open. One other table was occupied, and that was across the room from where we sat. After the waitress disappeared into the kitchen with our order, Hon got up and walked around to look at the pictures hanging on the walls. They were all Chesapeake scenes from the past, marshes full of geese or sailboats working on the Bay. He studied each of them before he sat down again.

"Glenn," he said, "I can't write that book. I don't have the slightest idea how to start a project like that. The only writin' I've done in the past twenty years has been checks, and some of them haven't been any good. If you'll write it, I'll help all I can."

I thought back to how much time I put into the book I had recently completed. For almost a year I had come home from the office every day, eaten supper, and stayed up half the night writing. Virginia and I nearly abandoned our social life during that time. We didn't even turn on the television while I was working, because it distracted me. To write a book while holding down a full time job is more than just a passing notion, that I had learned. I hated to say no, but....

The waitress slid a couple of plates of spaghetti onto the table in front of us. We were hungry enough that we didn't notice if it was tasty or not, we just gobbled it down. Afterward, as we stepped out of the restaurant into the chilly night air, a flock of geese passed directly overhead, honking their way toward the river.

"Geese spend a lot of their days inland now, in the corn fields," Hon said. "They used to feed on the grass in the shallows, you know, but with it gone they had to find somethin' else to eat. Canvasbacks and red heads and widgeons don't like the corn fields, though, so they've become pretty scarce. You hardly see one of them anymore."

As I pulled out onto the highway, Hon reclined his seat as far back as he could.

"Wake me up when we get to Crisfield," he said. "And swing by the creek on the way home. I need to look at the boat."

I woke up at dawn the next morning, dressed, and quietly slipped out the door. The morning promised to be beautiful and I felt like walking a long way, so I turned toward town.

First, I passed the modest houses along our road. Watermen had built their homes there on the edge of the marsh near the creek so they could be within walking distance of their boats. The land was barely above sea level, low enough that storm tides frequently covered it with sea water, and the mosquitos were so thick in the summer that a normal person couldn't stand to live there. But watermen were not normal people. Mosquitos and storms and high tides didn't bother them at all.

After I passed the tiny watermen's community, I entered a pine woods. The pines were a sign that the land was higher, that the tides didn't cover it as often. When I emerged from the woods, I turned left onto a new road that cut across a low strip of marsh to Somers Cove, where the state had recently built a marina to boost the town's sagging economy. This cove looked different when I was a boy. Then, it was a graveyard for big wooden sailboats, the schooners and bugeyes that were abandoned when the oysters faded out in the Bay. Beyond the marina, about a dozen seafood houses lined the waterfront. They handled a few oysters in the winter, but the summer crab season was what kept them going nowadays. Behind them, where other oyster houses once stood so close together that a man pushing a wheelbarrow could barely squeeze through the alleys, stretched silent parking lots paved with shells.

I next came to Maryland Avenue, a four lane highway that passed through the center of town and abruptly ended at the city dock. A two lane road and a railroad track once ran side by side here, but the tracks were pulled up and sold for scrap when the railroad went bankrupt. Beside this road, where freight company offices once enjoyed a booming business shipping train loads of seafood to the cities of the northeast and the midwest, a few restaurants and souvenir shops silently waited for tourists to trickle in next summer.

I made my way to the end of the road, to the pavilion that was built there after the big freight terminal rotted away and then burned. On these docks that separated the firm ground of the Eastern Shore from the waters of the Chesapeake, the town of Crisfield was born. The only reason the town ever existed was because of its docks, and because of all the oysters and fish and crabs that passed over them. And now that the oysters and the fish were nearly gone, there was hardly any reason for the town to be here at all.

The docks were not busy like they used to be, but to me this was still a fine place to come in the morning. I enjoyed spending time by myself near the water, it seemed to wash out the confusion that had cluttered my mind, it helped me bring life back into a proper perspective. Too bad I couldn't do it more often, more than just an hour or two a year.

I looked at the water beneath my feet. The choppy waves slowly rolled in before the breeze and dashed against the pilings. They were clean and beautiful. I thought back to when this harbor would have been littered with half sunken barrels and boards and cartons and great bunches of floating grass. People in town used to think of the harbor as the city dump. Anything they didn't want they just threw overboard and let the next ebbing tide carry it out. People don't do that anymore. Today's clean water laws don't permit it.

That explained why no barrels or trash were bobbing in the water, but what about the grass? People never threw the grass overboard. It grew there naturally, and floated to the surface when it died. Great bunches of it used to drift along with the tides, bunches so thick that they looked like little islands with birds walking on them. If you didn't notice a bunch and ran over it with your boat, it could foul the propeller and even stop up the water pump, and then your motor would overheat. But now, I didn't see any grass at all. I didn't see any floating in the harbor, and I didn't even see any between the docks in front of the restaurant where it always used to get trapped and pile up.

Maybe Hon was right. No grass in the water, no life in the water.

Virginia and I got off to an early start for home Sunday morning. As we drove along the seventeen mile bridge that crosses the mouth of the Chesapeake, I mentioned that we were well ahead of our normal schedule and could spend a few hours sightseeing. I had always wanted to visit the Mariner's

28

Museum in Newport News, and this would be a good chance for that. Virginia dug through the glove compartment, located a map, and guided us around Norfolk and across the James River to the museum. We found an impressive building set deep into a heavily wooded park. As we entered the front door, an enormous golden eagle that once decorated the bow of an American fighting frigate stared down at us. In awe, I stood there and looked around at the vast display of exhibits, trying to determine where we should begin.

To our right was a huge room with a sign that announced *The Chesapeake Bay, a Way of Life*. That was the place for us to start. I didn't want to miss anything in the room. I began by examining the maps on the wall just to the left of the entry. A placard beside the oldest map proclaimed that it was drawn in 1719. I looked at the Crisfield area to see what towns were there. Only one settlement was marked. To my surprise, it was named Damned Quarter. That was one of the pirate towns Hon had mentioned.

"Born to be a man, but died a grocer."

I couldn't remember where I had heard that phrase, but it kept repeating in my mind as I drove home from the office in the bumper-to-bumper beltline traffic. An image from my childhood memories appeared along with the phrase, that of a balding man with a stained butcher's apron wrapped around his ample waist, standing behind a counter ready to pick a can of beans or a jar of pickles from the shelves that lined the wall, or whack a couple of pork chops off the big slab he kept handy in his glass fronted meat case. He was judged as a prosperous man in our little community at that time, but that did not mean he enjoyed a great income. The standard against which we measured a man's prosperity had sunk very low since oysters became scarce in the Bay.

His family's lifestyle, however, sparkled with ambience that a waterman's wife could only dream about—a car, central heat, running water, and one of the first television sets in town. I didn't know of any waterman on the creek, though, who would trade places with him.

Instead of butcher's aprons I wore pin striped suits, but still I felt linked to this hapless grocer by occupation. Whereas he had chosen to spend his life buried behind a counter, between the big glass jar of pickled pigs feet to his right hand side and the candy case to his left, so I had doomed myself to sitting behind a desk piled high with paperwork for projects that would become obsolete and forgotten in just a few years.

To carry the similarity further, I could not recall ever detecting a tinge of regret in Hon's face the few times I heard him compare his circumstances with mine.

Virginia knew how discouraged I could become about work, so when I dragged myself into the house she had the dinner table set and a smile on her face. Her cheerfulness made me feel as though I might somehow be able to salvage something worthwhile from the day.

"A letter came for you," she said as she stepped into the kitchen. "It's beside the lamp."

I picked up the envelope and looked at the return address. It was from a Mr. Milton, of Knoxville, Tennessee. I had never heard of him, so I wondered what could be inside. I tore the envelope open and found a note. It was a response to an inquiry I had sent to a genealogical newsletter, asking for help in tracing my ancestors.

"The following may be of interest to you. From *The*

General Historie of Virginia, New England, and the Summer Isles, by Captain John Smith, (originally written in the early 1600s) a Thomas Lawson is listed as an adventurer for Virginia. He is also referred to as Captain Thomas Lawson in *A Voyage to Virginia*."

The next sheet of paper was a photocopy of a page from John Smith's book, describing how the settlers at Jamestown were divided into five companies, and Thomas Lawson was captain of one of them. I remembered that John Smith came to the Virginia colony in 1607 with the first group of settlers, and that he returned to England in 1609. He immediately began to write about life in the colonies, a topic of great interest in Europe at that time, and here on the pages of two of his books was evidence that our family legend was based on fact.

A few weeks later, a large envelope came from Hon. I tore it open and found a book titled *The Bounty of the Chesapeake*. Bob Lippson, the marine biologist from the Easton show, had sent it to Hon, and he had immediately forwarded it to me. I opened the book to see what it was about. It was a collection of excerpts from letters the early colonists sent back to England.

I sat down and began to read the fascinating firsthand accounts of what life was like along the Chesapeake in the early sixteen hundreds, during the days of Thomas Lawson. The letters told of sixty-eight sturgeon taken with a single sweep of a net. They told of the Indians making a dugout canoe by hollowing the trunk of a huge tree with fire and scraping the coals out with shells.

Other letters told how the colonists carelessly laid their

fishing nets on the beach to rot instead of hanging them to dry. That winter they ran out of food. One small band of men asked for permission to take the best boat and remaining nets to the mouth of the Bay to fish. They never returned to the fort. Instead, they sailed off to become pirates. The colonists were turned out of the fort to forage for themselves. Only sixty of them lived through that winter. They did so by eating the oysters they picked up in the shallow waters along the shores of the James River.

In later years, the colonists collected oysters during the summer and dumped them into shallow creeks in case the food supplies ran low during the winter. My grandfather did the same when I was a boy. When the weather became severe and he didn't have any income, he walked to the creek where he had built his bed of oysters and brought back a basketful. My grandmother fried them, or stewed them with onions and potatoes, or baked them in a deep pan with a crust like a pie.

For variety during those lean times, my grandfather sometimes took his spade to the creek and dug a bucket of thin shelled clams that he called mananose. I had never heard clams called by that name except along the Bay, so I picked up my dictionary and searched for the word. I found it. It was an Indian word, from the Algonquin language. It meant 'to gather, to pick up.' I was struck by the realization that during my own life, our family had survived at times much the same way as Thomas Lawson and the other original Jamestown colonists.

"Virginia," I said, "someone needs to write a book that tells people just how much the Bay has changed, and how much we have lost."

Chapter 3
A Time of Plundering

Whenever Virginia and I drove to Crisfield, we wondered how we would find Floyd. His illness frustrated Margaret and baffled his doctor. Some days he would be fine, as though he had no problems except those that are inevitable with aging. Other times he was confused, and stumbled when he walked.

We also wondered about Hon, was he making enough money on the water to keep at it? If he left the water he might not be able to find work in Crisfield, and that would be unfortunate for all of us. If he had to take a job out of town, he could no longer run across the road whenever our parents needed help, and they needed it often now that Floyd was sick so much of the time.

When we arrived in November, we found that Floyd was staying in the house most of the time during the cold weather and was feeling fine, but Hon wasn't making out very well. Oysters were so scarce he had tied the boat up at the shanty. Margaret said he had purchased a mailing list of wildfowl art enthusiasts and spent about a thousand dollars to send out a brochure offering my book and a group of wildfowl art prints for sale, and now he was fixing up the old building next to his house. She viewed that as a rather reckless expenditure for someone who had not brought home any income since crabbing ended last summer and was just about broke.

I slipped on my jacket and walked across the road to see what Hon was doing. The old building used to be a tiny, one bedroom house. A waterman had lived alone there, but a few years ago he fell asleep in a chair while smoking and set the place on fire. The ceiling and the interior walls were all charred, the floor was burned through, and about one quarter of the roof was gone. The house never had running water and the lot was small, so there just wasn't much to interest a buyer when it was put up for sale. Hon bought it for next to nothing to use as a shed for storing his equipment. When I opened the door, I found him standing atop a mound of broken and charred plasterboard.

"Welcome to the home office of Chesapeake Art," he announced.

He had cleaned out all the old motor parts, the broken oyster tongs, and the baskets of crabpot buoys that once filled the building. He had patched the roof and the floor with sheets of plywood, and now he was ripping out the interior walls. He pointed to where he would put his desk when he found one, where he would store his inventory of books and prints, and where he would build a bench for wrapping packages. And eventually, he informed me, he would mat and frame pictures, as soon as he had the money to buy matting board and moldings.

"Let me show you somethin'," he said. He reached under a sheet of plastic, pulled out a carton, and proudly raised the cover to display a color print. I recognized that it had been made from a Lem Ward painting.

Hon pointed to the lower right edge. "See that," he said, "Lem's signature, by his own hand. There'll never be another one of those."

Lem was the wildfowl artist about whom I had written the book. His carvings became very valuable, but not until his most productive days were over. In his last years he was an invalid, confined to his bed and his wheelchair. His daughter, Ida, spent every day and every night caring for him at his home near Jenkins Creek. Were it not for her tireless efforts, he would have been placed in a nursing home. Lem's greatest concern at that time was for Ida's future, because his money was nearly spent out and she had little prospect of finding a job to support herself. An artist friend discovered that Lem had once painted wildfowl scenes on canvas and had given them away. He searched until he found several of these paintings, made prints of them, propped Lem up in his wheelchair to autograph them, and left them for Ida. Hon was selling the prints for her.

"I know the sales from one book and a few prints aren't much to depend on for a livin'," he said, "but that's all I have right now. Maybe I can make it 'til the weather warms up and crabbin' begins. I just hate the thought of workin' for someone else so long as I can possibly get by on my own."

He closed the carton and slipped it back under the plastic. "By the way," he said, "have you thought any more about writin' that book?"

"Yeah, I already started," I told him. "Right now, I'm trying to imagine how the early settlers in this area made their living. Take Hance, for example, I don't have the slightest idea what he did after he arrived here."

"I can help you with that," he said. "I'm pretty sure he was a waterman, even when he first came here, 'cause most of the land he bought was marsh. It wasn't any good for farmin', just huntin' and fishin'."

"But where did he sell his fish?"

"He sold some of 'em locally. Everybody who lived here didn't fish then, any more than they do now. What he had left over, he probably salted and shipped to Baltimore."

"Where did he get his salt?" I asked.

"He probably made his own. The process was simple, all

he needed was salt water and an evaporatin' pond. He had both, livin' where he did near the head of the creek. For the pond, he merely scraped the shallow layer of topsoil off the clay and threw up a bank around the perimeter. He filled it at the peak of the incomin' tide. When that water evaporated, he filled it again, and when enough salt accumulated he scraped it up and stored it in a keg."

"Interesting."

"Would you like to see a salt pond?" Hon asked.

"Yes!"

"Let's go to the Circle Inn tomorrow mornin', Carroll Adams eats breakfast there. He lives on an old colonial farm with a salt pond."

When we walked through the door of the Circle Inn the next morning, Carroll was sitting at his usual table eating his usual breakfast of scrambled eggs and toast with orange marmalade. We sat down with him, and when the waitress came over I ordered an omelet with toast and orange marmalade.

"You're only the second person to ever ask for marmalade here," she told me.

"They bought it especially for me," Carroll said. He looked up at the waitress and instructed her, "You can let him have some."

Hon asked Carroll if he would take us back to the salt pond.

"This may not be the best time," Carroll replied. "It's way out back of the house, and this is deer hunting season, you know."

"Can you sing?" Hon asked.

"Not very well," Carroll replied.

"You don't have to be good, just loud," Hon said. "I want everybody within a quarter mile to know we're there."

We arranged to meet Carroll at his farm later that day, but a light drizzle set in shortly afterward, so we abandoned that plan and spent the next couple of hours at Hon's shop instead, with him telling me what he had learned about the way Hance lived.

"A farmer could get rich by growin' tobacco," he said. "Tobacco was money, they paid their bills and their taxes with it. If a farmer today could grow money, do you think he'd bother with carin' for cattle and hogs, and curin' the meat?"

Hon went on to explain the implications of such a tobacco oriented farm economy. Specialized food providers were necessary to help feed the barrel makers and the blacksmiths and the schooner captains, and that was how Hance fit into the picture. He was a waterman, a hunter, and a fisherman. He built his house at the head of Jenkins Creek, near the farm lands where his customers worked and lived, and also convenient to the hunting marshes and the sheltered waters of the Little Annemessex River.

Hance spent the summer and fall fishing and raking up oysters in the river. The fish that he did not immediately sell he salted away in barrels, and he dumped the oysters into the creek near the house because they would not become fat and tasty until winter. When the weather turned cold and migrating wildfowl flocked to the marshes, he hunted ducks to sell along with the salted fish and the oysters he was catching from the river, and when the weather turned really foul, so bad he didn't dare venture out of the harbor in his boat, he tonged up the oysters he had dumped into the creek near his house and he sold them.

Hance surely owned a fast sailboat, most likely a log canoe, because that was by far the most popular boat on the Bay during his time. The colonists had copied the Indian's log canoe, for they found that it was a very sensible and durable boat, though it was crudely constructed. With their metal tools, however, the colonists vastly improved on the Indian version. They sharpened the bow and the stern so it would slip through the water more effortlessly, they flattened the bottom so it would not be as tippy, and they added a sail so the wind would do most of the work for them.

This canoe was their chief means of travel throughout the tidewater settlements of colonial Virginia and Maryland, because traveling on land was hindered by lack of roads and by the many tidal creeks that penetrated deeply into the forested shoreline. Every settlement, no matter how tiny, was beside a creek or a river, and nearly all commerce in these two colonies was by way of this highway system, the Chesapeake Bay and its many watery fingers.

So Hance needed a boat like the canoe, not only for fishing and oystering, but also for trips to Somers Cove, the nearest deep water port community and his link to the rest of the world. There, ships from Baltimore and Norfolk anchored in the well protected harbor, and merchants along the waterfront bought his salted fish and sold him tools and ropes and fabrics, and whatever else he needed for work and for the home.

When the War for Independence began, Hance was about fifty years old, but he still joined the home guard. Samuel, his son by his second wife, an Indian, joined with him. The home guard was a company of local men whose purpose was to defend the towns along the shores of the Bay. Their enemy was not the British soldiers, but the picaroons, the Bay pirates.

The picaroons had been an irritation ever since the mid sixteen hundreds. Living as they did on the islands along the edge of the Tangier Sound, they could not be policed by any land bound force. British naval patrols had kept them under reasonable control, but they still darted out and seized a small trading ship whenever they had the chance, then slipped back into their shallow harbors and hid their boats among the trees. When the war broke out, the British contracted with them to secure supplies for the army and licensed them to disrupt patriot shipping. The picaroons raided farms and carried off the grain and cattle to feed the army of Lord Cornwallis, and they also took advantage of the wartime emergency and their British protection to plunder rampantly throughout the Bay.

Working from their towns of Damned Quarter, Devil Island, and Rogues Point, they struck so swiftly that the patriot's defenses rarely saw them. They controlled the waters of the central Chesapeake, so no assault could be mounted against their island bases. They spread such fear throughout the Bay that few captains dared to venture out of harbor, so the picaroons then boldly began to attack port cities. They captured ships right at the docks, sailed them to their islands, then outfitted them for their own use or sold them to the British. They even attacked one boat yard and burned a ship that Maryland was building to use against them, and they recklessly plundered farther and farther inland.

The situation of the patriots who lived on the lower Eastern Shore of Maryland became desperate. Their commerce with the other parts of the colony had always been by water, but now they were under a total blockade, for any ship coming to their ports had to sail right past the picaroon islands and would certainly be captured. The residents of Somerset County knew they would get no help from the beleaguered colonial government, so they raised enough money by public subscription to finance a ship for their own defense. They built it at Snow Hill, far up the narrow Pocomoke River, where the picaroons could not venture without exposing themselves to musket fire from the wooded shore.

The ship they built was a sailing barge, very wide and with a shallow draft so it could carry a tremendous expanse of sail and still be able to pursue the picaroons into the shoals around their island bases. With its crew of local watermen, the *Protector*, as the barge was named, soon drove the picaroons from the Pocomoke Sound and even captured several of their vessels as prizes. The other counties on the Eastern Shore were so encouraged by the success of the *Protector* that they built their own barges, and fitted out suitable ships that the *Protector* had captured from the picaroons.

The picaroons, however, were not easily intimidated. They kept up with the locations of the patrol vessels and continued their raids elsewhere, even after Cornwallis surrendered and the war ended. The governor of Maryland called on the French fleet, which had driven off the mighty British navy, to help control the raiders, but they had little effect because their deep draft ships could not follow the swift picaroons into their shoal water refuges.

The Maryland Assembly passed legislation calling for a naval force to be raised to eliminate the picaroons from the Bay. The *Protector* and the other county defense ships were placed under the command of this navy, and began a systematic patrol of the waters where the picaroons were operating. Five months after this navy was formed, six of its patrol ships entered the Tangier Sound to stalk six raiders known to be operating there. They found the picaroon ships at Kedges Straits, a shallow thoroughfare between the Tangier Sound and the Chesapeake Bay, just to the north of Smith Island. With no battle plan except to engage the enemy and destroy them, the naval ships attacked the picaroons. The *Protector* forged ahead of the other ships, getting between them and the picaroons and preventing them from being able to fire at the enemy. A cartridge on the *Protector* broke open, spreading powder all over the deck, and a spark from a cannon ignited it. Fire flashed across the deck, exploding other cartridges and setting the ship ablaze. When the other naval captains saw the explosion aboard their command ship, they turned tail and ran. The picaroons rammed two of their barges against the flaming ship and swarmed aboard. They slaughtered most of the crew in a furious hand-to-hand battle as the other four raiders chased after the five fleeing naval vessels.

The picaroons again controlled the Bay, and were free to plunder as they chose. But not for long. They were soon subdued, not by naval ships or by soldiers carrying guns, but by Bible toting Methodist preachers.

When I left Hon's shop that morning, I had a much better vision of how Hance and his neighbors struggled to feed their families and defend their independence. I also realized that Hon had awakened a lot of memories that had been dormant for years. I especially thought back to how the old timers used to sit by their shanties at the creek and tell what had been passed on to them about those early Methodist preachers. They must have been extraordinary men, for in just a few years they converted entire communities of rugged picaroons and watermen who had laughed at any attempt to impose authority over them, and who respected few men other than their own kind. The remarkable influence of these preachers was not temporary, either. A full two centuries later, the descendants of these people were still studying the Bible on a daily basis and directing their lives according to its teachings.

I knew a book had been written about one of these preachers, so I drove through the drizzle to the Crisfield library to search it out. When I inquired at the front desk, the librarian led me to the reference section and pulled a small book from a shelf. She told me it had been out of print for a long time, but it was still very popular there, and since they only had one copy she could not allow me to check it out. She pointed me to a comfortable chair beside a lamp.

The cloth binding of the cover was frazzled and held on with tape, and the pages were yellowed with age. The book was worn, but not abused. It had obviously been treated with respect. I opened the cover to reveal the title, *Parson of the Islands*, by Adam Wallace, 1861.

I settled down in the chair, turned the page, and began to read the story of Joshua Thomas, the most famous preacher to ever serve on the Chesapeake Bay.

Joshua was born in 1776. I noted that Hance was about fifty years older, so I should be able to discover much about how he and his neighbors lived by reading this story.

Joshua was a small child when his father died of infection. His mother left their home on the mainland of the Maryland Eastern Shore and sought refuge with relatives on Tangier Island, about fifteen miles from where Hance lived and just over the state line into Virginia. She married a somewhat prosperous islander, and they bought a house near the beach. Shortly after they moved in, a band of sea raiders came ashore at their house, looted it, and burned it to the ground. Joshua's stepfather never recovered from that blow and began to drink heavily. He fell out of his sailboat while drunk and he drowned, leaving the family destitute.

Joshua was merely a boy, but the responsibility for feeding the family fell heavily on him. He quickly mastered the skills of a waterman and by the time his head came up to a man's shoulders, he was already known as the best fisherman and the most skillful boatman on the island.

While Joshua was fishing near Tangier one spring day, three schooners came into sight from the north. As these boats worked their way toward him, he could see that passengers crowded the decks. One of the boats came alongside, and the captain offered to purchase all the fish he had caught. Joshua agreed, and the captain then asked if they could hire him to pilot them to Pungoteague. Joshua replied that he would be happy to do so in the morning. They agreed to that arrangement, and he led them to Tangier to anchor just offshore for the night.

That evening, the passengers on the schooners began to sing and pray and praise God. The islanders had never seen such a spectacle. They congregated on the nearby beach, listening and watching in amazement until the singing finally died down late at night.

The next day, Joshua and a friend set out in a sailing canoe to lead the schooners to Pungoteague, where they found a great many other boats anchored and a huge crowd of people gathered on the shore. The passengers on the schooners persuaded Joshua and his friend to stay awhile and attend what they called a Methodist camp meeting. Joshua was astonished at what he saw in that meeting, for ordinary looking men were praying without a book and preaching without a written sermon, and everyone seemed as unaccountably happy as the passengers on the schooners had been.

Like most of the other islanders, Joshua and his friend

belonged to the Episcopal Church, which had been the official church of the colony of Virginia. Since their church held no meetings on Tangier, they had to sail to the mainland when they wanted to attend a worship service. Even in the best of weather, this all day trip was hardly worth the effort just to listen to a robed priest read a prepared message full of words they did not understand. So their contacts with the church were infrequent, at the best. Nevertheless, being joyous at a religious meeting seemed such a sacrilege that Joshua's friend became extremely uneasy and demanded they immediately leave that place, for he feared God was going to send an earthquake to swallow everyone there. Joshua returned to the boat with him, and they sailed back to Tangier.

But Joshua made up his mind to go to the next camp meeting, which was to be held at a place he called Anne-messex. He asked several neighbors to go with him, but they all feared they would become contaminated by attending, so he sailed alone to the mainland on the Friday the meeting was to begin. He found a large and orderly crowd there, worshiping solemnly and listening intently to the words of the speaker. When the speaker finished, the congregation sang several hymns and another speaker began. And so the meeting carried on through the day, with sermons about the consequences of sin and exhortations to repent and be saved, and with prayers and hymns. Occasionally, one or two or even a small cluster of people walked forward through the crowd to kneel at the mourners bench, where the eyes of the whole congregation would be fixed upon them. Joshua felt an urging from within, but he had no intention of making such a public spectacle of himself.

The meeting resumed Saturday. After a full day of sermons and exhortations, Joshua began to feel so uneasy he left the crowd and went alone into the woods.

During the Sunday meeting, a great many people were overcome by their emotions. Some stood up and shouted that they had been born again from above, others fell to the ground and rolled around, or lay as if they were dead. Joshua left and went into the woods again, away from the crowd and the noise. He felt even more uneasy than before. From what he had seen in the meeting that day, he wondered if the secret to this being wondrously born again might be in falling to the ground. So he picked out a smooth place that was free of stumps and roots, raised his hands to heaven, and fell flat of his back.

Fortunately, he didn't break any bones, but neither did he gain any feeling of comfort. So, after laying on the ground for a long while in hopes that God would eventually notice, he picked himself up and sneaked back to the meeting.

That evening, during the very last sermon, Joshua felt his strong will give up its demand to obtain faith in secret, so when the preacher ended the sermon and invited sinners to repent and be saved, Joshua arose and walked through the crowd to the mourners bench to kneel and pray.

When he returned to Tangier, Joshua began regular prayer meetings in his home for his family and neighbors. Under his leadership, the meetings grew in size and spread to the nearby islands. So many people were attending the prayer meetings at Smith Island that a camp meeting was called there, and a great crowd came by boats from Tangier and from the mainland to attend. According to Joshua, the opening sermon at this camp meeting was by an old preacher from Anne-messex, a long time defender of the Methodist faith named Hance Lawson.

I heard a noise and looked up from the book. There stood Virginia and Margaret.

"Glenn," Virginia said, "your mother and I have been looking all over town for you."

"The library is about to close," Margaret added. "We're going to town to start our Christmas shopping, we'll meet you at Kent's."

I didn't realize I had been reading so long. Reluctantly, I returned the book to the reference shelf and hoped it would still be there the next time I came back to Crisfield. I drove to Kent's and parked by the sidewalk right in front of the door. When I stepped inside, I found myself facing a rack of books. On the far right side of the top shelf, in a shiny white cover, stood *Parson of the Islands*.

"Virginia," I said as I picked up the book, "here's what you can get me for Christmas."

Following the War for Independence, markets for fish and oysters at cities such as Baltimore, Alexandria, and Norfolk made the Virginians who lived beside the Potomac River very unhappy about the location of the boundary line between their state and Maryland. When King Charles I granted the colony of Maryland to Charles Calvert and set the boundary along the Virginia shore of the Potomac, he gave the entire river to Maryland. For years, Virginia's leaders attempted to persuade the Marylanders to allow their residents equal right to fish and to catch oysters in the river. When they tired of this approach, they threatened to blockade the entrance of the Chesapeake Bay and tax all ships traveling to and from Maryland ports. Maryland, of course, objected strenuously, and the dispute was referred to President George Washington. From the Maryland point of view, he was not the best choice as an arbitrator. He called for each state to send their

46

representatives to meet with him at his Mount Vernon home overlooking the Potomac from the Virginia shore. There they agreed to a settlement. Ships to and from Maryland were guaranteed free passage, Virginia and Maryland residents were granted equal fishing rights in the Potomac and the Pocomoke rivers that marked the boundaries between the states, and the boundary line that crossed the Bay was adjusted northward to give Virginia a larger share of the water and the oyster beds.

"Oysters used to be so plentiful around here they were a menace to navigation," Hon said as he turned up the kerosene heater in his shop. "Great mounds of 'em grew like the coral reefs of tropical seas. The captains called these mounds 'oyster rocks', and they had to constantly watch out for 'em because if a ship ran aground on one, the waves could easily pound it up and down until it burst open like a ripe watermelon. And now, I can't be sure I'll find enough oysters in a day to pay my boat expenses, let alone bring a little cash home. The problem started about the year eighteen hundred, when the New England schooner captains sailed into the Bay."

These schooner captains had already cleaned the oysters out of Long Island Sound in an attempt to satisfy the New Englander's appetites and their own desire for wealth. Of course, they accomplished neither objective, so they descended upon the oyster rich Chesapeake Bay, bringing with them their terribly efficient harvester, the dredge. This was a heavy iron rake four or five feet wide, with teeth several inches long and a chain link bag. As they pulled a dredge behind their boat, its teeth dug a swath across the oyster rock, broke the oysters free, and scooped them into the bag.

A powerful schooner could pull three or four dredges at once. A schooner had a winch bolted to each side of the deck, with four men slaving to crank it by hand. When a dredge filled, which took only a few minutes, the crew cranked it up to the side of the ship, hauled it onto the deck, and dumped it while they sailed along dragging the other dredges.

"This was back breakin' work," Hon said. "The Chesapeake watermen that the schooner captains hired called it drudgin'. They claimed it was the most drudgerous work they knew."

No one knows how many millions of bushels of oysters these drudgers removed from the Bay and carried to New England, but the watermen did know that when a fleet finished working an oyster rock, they left little behind besides a few muddy shells. Mindful of what these schooners had done to the oysters in the Long Island Sound, the legislatures of the states of Virginia and Maryland both passed laws prohibiting the use of drudges in the Bay, and also prohibited the shipment of oysters from the Bay on boats except those owned by residents.

The New England schooner captains needed the oysters to keep their businesses going, so many of them moved to Baltimore. From there, they sailed down the Bay, anchored their schooners in protected harbors near where the watermen lived, and filled them in just a few days with oysters that the watermen caught. The state had only a few oyster policemen at that time, enough to watch the big schooners but not nearly enough to control the thousands of watermen, many of whom had been picaroons and, though they now were Bible quoting Methodists and would not think of pillaging the properties of others, they felt the state had overstepped its authority when it began to tell them how to catch oysters. The watermen had their blacksmiths make small drudges they could haul aboard by hand, and continued the plundering of the oyster bars.

Who could catch oysters and how, and where the boundary line should be suddenly faded from importance in 1812, when the sails of the mighty British navy appeared again in the Bay. Their ships landed an army that brushed aside the American defenses at Bladensburg, burned the new capital of Washington, and took Alexandria without resistance. The troops then sailed to the island of Tangier to rest and prepare for an attack on the city of Baltimore.

Tangier did not have a government like other cities in the country at that time. They had no elected or appointed officials, no law officers, no judges. Every man did as he saw fit, which would seem to lead to anarchy and confusion, but this was not the case on the little island, for the people there settled any dispute among themselves by referring to the Bible and doing what they thought was right in the sight of God. Their one acknowledged leader was the preacher, Joshua Thomas, and it was he who stood on the beach to meet the first British officers as they came ashore.

Joshua appealed to them to not garrison their troops at the grove of trees where the islanders held their camp meetings, for they considered that place to be sacred ground. The officers agreed, and had the soldiers pitch their tents alongside the grove instead. Even though the British considered the islanders to be prisoners of war, all the time they were on Tangier they treated the residents with respect, and any official dealings they had with the people they carried through Joshua.

As the British prepared to break camp and sail for Baltimore, the commander of the army troops asked Joshua to preach for them. This commander probably was familiar with the practices of the government controlled Church of England, and expected Joshua to invoke God's blessings upon them in the coming battle.

Joshua, however, served a different authority.

With twelve thousand soldiers standing at attention before him at the campground and an officer bearing a sword on each side of him, Joshua began his message. He followed the same basic outline he used whenever he preached. With his open Bible in his hand, he told them that all men were sinners in the sight of God, and that the penalty for their sin was to be cast into a fiery hell when their time on this earth was finished. Then he told them how he had once been doomed to that eternal place of torment himself, but that God had provided a way of escape. He told them that God loved sinners like himself so much that He sent Jesus Christ into the world to save them, and that he had accepted Jesus as his Savior and was now assured of a heavenly home. Then he shouted to the mass of troops standing before him that each of them needed to repent as he had done, and prepare themselves to meet their final Judge, for God had told him to warn them that they would never take Baltimore, and many of them would die in the attempt.

Joshua closed his Bible and bowed his head, wondering if he would be killed on the spot. But the British didn't say a word to him. The officers marched the silent troops to the beach where they boarded the launches that were waiting to row them to the warships. As soon as the last launch was hoisted on deck, the British fleet weighed anchor and sailed from Tangier, bound up the Bay toward the city of Baltimore, and the fort named McHenry that guarded the entrance to its harbor.

Several days later, when the sails of the fleet appeared

again, Joshua returned to his station at the beach to meet the first British launch as it ground ashore. When the officer stepped from the launch, Joshua asked him if they had taken Baltimore. The officer replied that they had not, and that many of their men had been killed, including the commanding general.

The troops came ashore again to encamp beside the grove until they received further orders from England. Several soldiers sought out Joshua and told him that as a result of his preaching they had made their peace with God.

During their stay on the island, the British soldiers were sent ashore on the mainland several times to plunder small towns and farms in search of food. One of these raids was directed at Jenkins Creek, but a Tangier waterman who learned of the plan sailed his small skiff across the sound to warn the people there. The farmers and the watermen who lived nearby, such as Samuel Lawson and his son, William, threw up a barricade of timber and farm carts at the landing and stationed themselves behind it with their rifles.

The water at the mouth of the creek was so shallow that the warship could not get close enough to bring the barricade within range of its heavy guns. The troops boarded naval launches and were rowed into the creek, but they could not go ashore to assault the defenders because the banks of the creek were all marsh, so soft they could not walk without bogging down to their waists in the mud. The raiding party turned back and boarded their ship to return to Tangier. Shortly afterward, the British on the island were informed that the war had ended and they sailed from the Bay.

Joshua Thomas eventually moved to Devil Island, the old picaroon settlement close to the mainland. There, he pastored a church while he earned his living by fishing, just as he had on Tangier. Soon, every adult in that community, and most of those throughout all the islands in the central Chesapeake, were added to the roles of the Methodist Church. To show their change of heart, the islanders renamed their towns. Devil Island, which the old timers pronounced Dea'vil Island, became known as Deal Island. Damned Quarter became Dames Quarter, and Rogues Point was renamed Rhodes Point after a famous missionary.

To get about better among the island churches, Joshua purchased a log canoe that he named *The Methodist*. This canoe was about twenty-six feet long and five feet wide, one of two canoes carved from the same tree by a man who lived at Annemessex. With this canoe, Joshua continued for many years to sail throughout the islands, carrying the Word of God to his flock of rugged watermen.

"Glenn," Margaret said, "your father shouldn't be driving his car, but I can't get him to give it up. I'm afraid he's going to kill somebody."

I talked to Floyd, and reasoned with him for nearly an hour, and finally he agreed that he shouldn't drive any more. At least, I thought he did. But shortly afterward I looked out and his car wasn't in the driveway. Margaret said he had driven it to the barber shop.

I walked across the road to see Hon for a brotherly conference.

"Yeah, I know," he said. "I've been talkin' to him about not drivin', and about not usin' his power tools any more. He won't quit though. He views losin' them the same as losin' his independence. Reasonin' won't work, because he refuses to admit the seriousness of his condition."

"What'll we do? We can't let him kill somebody or hurt himself."

"I'll take care of it," Hon grumbled. "It's always me that ends up with the dirty work."

By noon the next day, Virginia and I had our clothes packed and were ready to start the drive back home. As we sat down at the table to have our lunch, I could see something was troubling Floyd. I asked what was wrong.

"I don't know what I'm going to do about Hon," he said. "This morning he came and borrowed my car. He's already borrowed my chain saw and my electric saw—and he never brings anything back."

Chapter 4
A Time of Plenty

Our son, Jamie, was finishing his junior year in college, but even though his grade point average in electrical engineering was good he had not been able to find a summer job where he could put his training to use. The only offers he had were as a framing carpenter or as the mate on Hon's crabbing boat. He decided to go crabbing. Though it did not pay as well as the construction job, he figured that working on a boat would be a lot more enjoyable than hammering nails in the burning sun. I was happy with his choice, because it would give him his first and possibly his only taste of how our family had earned their living for so many generations.

Virginia and Jamie and I drove into Crisfield just at the edge of dark on Friday. The town was a real mess. Empty bottles and cans and tree branches were strewn all about. When we pulled into Floyd's driveway, we found that the boards he kept stored in a pile behind his workshop were spread across the back yard. We stepped into the house to find the carpets rolled up and a web of extension cords strung between all the lamps and appliances. Margaret told us a severe storm had pushed the tide so high that salt water had come within an inch of covering the living room floor. It ruined most of the electrical circuits under the house and got into her car motor and the lawn mower. Hon fared even worse. It flooded his car and his pickup truck and several smaller motors, and it scattered the pilings he had stacked at the shanty to fix the rotting wharf. Margaret said Hon had been so busy cleaning up the flood damage that he had not been able to get the shanty and the boat ready for crabbing, but he was going to set his pots overboard on Saturday, anyway. He needed to start bringing some money home to pay the bills.

Jamie was to stay at Hon's house while he was working on the boat, so we carried his bags across the road. Hon's front yard was so squishy that we both got our feet wet even though we were trying to walk just on the high spots. We stepped through the front door to find the living room piled up with crab pot buoys he had brought in so they wouldn't float away. Hon, obviously tired to the bone, was stretched out in his reclining chair with a half empty glass of iced tea in his hand, his forearms and shirt and even his face were smeared with grease from a motor he was trying to salvage.

"Jamie," he said, looking up from his recliner, "I'm glad you decided to come and work on the water this summer. I'm going to teach you all I know about crabbin', 'cause I don't want you to have to depend on just electrical engineerin' to earn a livin'."

Before dawn the next morning, Jamie began his summer job on the Bay. When I walked to the shanty a little before noon, I found the boat back at the dock with him and Hon down in the hold and transmission parts spread all around them. They worked until dark before they had it reassembled. When the first rays of the sun gleamed across the Pocomoke Sound the following morning they were fishing their pots again, and had not returned to the shanty when Virginia and I left for the drive back home.

We returned to Crisfield two weeks later, mostly to see how Jamie was getting along. We found him stretched out on Hon's sofa, trying to steal a few minutes of rest before supper. I asked him how he liked crabbing.

"I never worked such long hours in my life," he said. "We

start at five every morning."

"What time do you finish?"

"We never finish."

He said that besides pulling the transmission apart twice during the first week, they hauled the boat up on the marine railway one evening, strung electric lights all around it and painted it, and were crabbing again the next morning. They had not missed a day of work yet.

"We still haven't caught up after that storm," Hon said, "but all we need to do now is replace the rotten pilings and boards in the wharf."

"That's not going to be as easy as it sounds," Jamie groaned. "They all look rotten to me."

Jamie was amazed at how many crabs they were catching.

"The first day out," he said, "we caught so many I figured there was no need to bother going back. But the next day, there were just as many again. There's no end to them."

"That's the same way people used to feel about oysters and fish and ducks," Hon said. "There were so many that everybody believed they were limitless. That was back in the glory days of the Bay seafood industry."

Those glory days began when the British pulled their ships out of the Chesapeake following the War of 1812, allowing the ports of Baltimore and Annapolis and Alexandria and Norfolk to build up a flourishing trade. Factories and warehouses popped up like weeds around the docks, and workers flocked in from the farms and small villages to fill the plentiful jobs. As these cities grew, so did a new type of business, that of providing food for the people who lived there. Baltimore, with its rapidly expanding population and its nearness to the industrial cities springing up in central and western Pennsylvania, became the best market for seafood on the Bay. Oysters, which were not so perishable as fish, became the favorite seafood for the merchants to deal in. During the fall and winter, schooners crowded against each other at the Baltimore docks waiting their turn to unload, while a steady stream of wagons piled high with oysters straight from the boats rumbled across the cobble stone streets, bound for places as far away as Pittsburgh. Ships also sailed from the harbor daily, hauling loads of Chesapeake oysters to New York, and to Boston and other New England ports.

As business grew in the northern and western cities, Baltimore merchants began to look to canning as a more convenient way to sell their oysters. The process was in its early stages of development at that time. It consisted of merely packing the containers full of raw food and sealing them so no air could get inside. This did little to preserve freshness, but a cumbersome bushel of oysters could be packaged in a one gallon container, which cost much less to ship. Since freight charges accounted for a large part of the price in the distant cities, the merchants there could now sell their oysters more cheaply and people bought more of them. So the Baltimore merchants opened shucking houses and canneries beside the docks, and hired the captains of sailing ships to scour the Bay for more oysters to accommodate their trade and to pay for their increased processing expenses.

William Lawson, who had occasionally earned cash by selling fish and oysters to the nearby villagers, found he could now make a steady living by selling to the ship captains who came regularly to Somers Cove. He no longer needed to live at the headwaters of Jenkins Creek, near the timber cutters and the tobacco farmers who had been his customers. Instead, he saw a distinct advantage to living as near the oyster bars as possible, because he could sell all he could catch.

A low ridge of solid land known as Hammock Point stuck out prominently into the Little Annemessex River just a short distance from Jenkins Creek. This land was high enough above sea level for trees to grow there, but it could not be reached by a horse drawn wagon because it was surrounded by a marsh on the eastern side and the river on the western side. The lack of a dry land trail made the property of little value to most people, but this presented no problem to William because he traveled mostly by boat along what had once been the colonial highway, the creeks and rivers and sounds that were still the main connection between the settlements along the Eastern Shore. William figured that Hammock point would be an ideal place for him to live, so he bought it. He spent one whole summer hauling bricks and lumber and shingles on his sailboat, and building a house there for his family.

William planted an orchard behind the house, and spaded up a vegetable garden. He did not move to Hammock Point to farm, though, because he was a waterman. On winter days when the weather was decent, William took his son, Samuel, and sailed out from the little creek beside the point into the river to tong up a boat load of oysters right in front of his house. He then sailed to Somers cove, sold his catch to a buy boat captain, and was home again before dark with his boat tied up just a few steps from the kitchen door. On days when the wind was blowing too hard to work out on the river, he poled his skiff into the marsh behind the house. Here the ducks were so thick they blotted out the sun like a cloud of smoke as they passed overhead. William and Samuel could kill more than a hundred on a good day. He took the ducks to Somers Cove and sold them to a buy boat captain, who packed them in barrels and carried them to Baltimore to peddle at the docks with his oysters.

I tried to imagine how important William's boat was to him. I supposed that it was as important as my car and my job combined were to me, for it was both his method of transportation and his way of earning a living. His boat was a log canoe, but it was far different than the one his grandfather Hance owned. Hance's canoe had been a fine craft, a vast improvement over the crude log troughs of the Indians. It was a sleek and nimble speedster, so streamlined that it slipped through the water leaving hardly a trace of a wake. But in the eighty years that had elapsed between the time Hance sailed from Virginia to Jenkins Creek and the time William sailed from there to live on Hammock Point, tremendous changes had taken place in the Chesapeake log canoe.

Many factors contributed to the rapid evolution in the design of this boat. For one, thousands of watermen were making them, and few had ever seen a set of plans or even a drawing. But they were all familiar with the canoe and what would be expected of it, because they spent most of their lives in and around the boats and knew very well which canoes were the best. Since the builders were often making the boats for their own use, they were more interested in improving the quality than in saving time or materials while building it. After all, they would hate to make a new canoe for themselves and then find that most of the others on their creek were faster and more seaworthy.

So the watermen took their time, carefully examining other canoes and trying to imitate or even improve on the best qualities of each as they built their own. Even if a waterman intended to exactly duplicate another canoe, he could not. Boats made from molds or from the same set of plans can be very nearly identical. But these canoes were hand carved from different trees, shaped with strokes of a broadaxe and an adz.

They were all different, and as a result their sailing qualities were different. The differences that improved the boats were copied, the others were ignored. It was these differences, whether by intention or by necessity or by accident, that sped up the evolution of the log canoe.

Not only had the design of the log canoe changed since Hance carved his, the size had changed also. A builder with a knack for engineering learned to fit several logs together to make a bigger canoe. Other builders along the Bay adopted his techniques and soon were turning out canoes of their own, some made from two logs and some from three. The Jenkins Creek builders preferred the three log version, for watermen there needed the bigger boats so they could work in the wide waters of the Pocomoke and Tangier Sounds during rough weather.

To make a three log canoe, the builder first selected a large tree with a straight trunk for the keel log. He then found two trees with slight bows for the curved sides. He cut the trees and he shaped the logs right where they fell. Then, with the help of some watermen friends, he carried the logs to the creek where he laid them side by side. He took great pride in the logs fitting perfectly when he brought them together, even though they had been shaped hundreds of yards apart in the woods.

The builder braced the keel log and a side log together. He then sawed along the seam between the two logs, all the way from the forward end to the stern. As his saw trimmed the facing edges of the two logs, it left them perfectly matched so when he fastened them together they would fit tightly enough that not a drop of water would pass through the seam. Then, he bored a hole through the side log and into the keel. He made a wooden pin that fit snugly inside this hole. He sawed a slot in the end of the pin and stuck a tiny wedge into it. He then

Carving logs for canoe with adz

drove the pin, wedge first, into the hole through the side log and into the keel. When the wedge struck the bottom of the hole in the keel, it spread the pin and stuck it tight. He then split the outer end of the pin and drove a wedge into it, sticking it tightly in the side log. By the time he added a couple more wooden pins, he could no longer pry the logs apart. He fastened the other side log onto the keel the same way, then turned the hull over and added a small deck forward and another aft. He fastened a rudder to the stern, and then, just before he slid the canoe into the water, he mounted two masts in it, each raked back in the fashion of the Baltimore clipper.

Building up a canoe from several logs was far more difficult than just cutting a tree down and carving it to shape, so some watermen specialized in making these boats and selling them to others who were not such good craftsmen. Other watermen specialized in making masts and paddles, and still others made the triangular sails. Most watermen, though, were like William. They specialized only in catching oysters to sell to the buy boats.

In 1830, an exciting event took place in the outskirts of Baltimore. An ironwright named Peter Cooper built a tiny steam engine with boiler tubes made of gun barrels. He mounted it on wheels, named it *Tom Thumb*, and arranged to race it against a stagecoach horse. The news spread through the city, and a great crowd turned out to watch the strange spectacle. The horse won the race, but nevertheless, the onlookers had witnessed the beginning of a revolution in land transportation.

Soon afterward, the Baltimore and Ohio Railroad began stretching tracks out of the port city toward the northeast and the growing midwest. This speedy and economical transportation opened up vast new markets for Baltimore merchants, especially for those who dealt with perishable products. They now could sell all the oysters they could get their hands on. New shucking houses opened in the many waterfront villages around the Bay, such as the one at Somers Cove. Shiny white paddlewheel steamers, their freight decks stuffed with cases of canned oysters, spread plumes of black smoke across the water as they raced between the villages and the city docks. Baltimore had firmly established itself as the oyster shipping capital of the world.

With all the money that could be made selling oysters to Baltimore, Samuel Lawson decided that he could afford his own boat. The builders at Jenkins Creek, where he had moved after he married, were making a new type of canoe that they called a brogan. It was carved from logs and pointed at each end like the time honored canoe, but it was much bigger. It was about forty feet long, made up of five logs fastened together with iron rods. It had two masts raked back much like those of his father's canoe, each carrying a triangular sail lashed to wooden hoops that slid up and down the mast. Unlike the canoe, it also sported a jib stretched from the top of the foremast to the tip of its bowsprit. Just behind the foremast stood a cabin that contained two bunks and a wood stove. A deck covered much of the boat to keep out the seas during rough weather.

With his new brogan, Samuel could work days that would have been too windy for the open canoe, and he could duck into the cabin during a squall or even sleep there when he could not get home for the night. The brogan soon paid for itself with the increased number of oysters he caught.

But then the Civil War broke out. Samuel and the other

watermen on the Chesapeake found themselves squarely between the two raging combatants. The northern half of the Bay was controlled by the Union, the southern half by the Confederacy. With each side struggling to possess this important waterway, no captain dared venture into the central Bay for fear of having his ship seized by the opposing navy. With their oyster business cut off altogether, many watermen turned to another way of making money, smuggling goods to the Confederacy.

Unscrupulous northern merchants, whose primary loyalty was to any profit they could make, hauled ropes and canvas and military supplies down the Eastern Shore. The watermen, who generally didn't care which side won the war, sneaked these goods aboard their log canoes and brogans that they kept hidden in the tree lined creeks near their houses. Benefited by the knowledge of a lifetime on these waters, they easily avoided the Union patrol boats by sailing the shallows at night until they were well down into Virginia, then they struck out across the open waters of the Bay to ports such as Hampton and Newport News to unload their contraband and collect their pay. In an attempt to stop this flow of supplies, the Union set up small encampments of soldiers on the Eastern Shore to watch the harbors and creeks. Any boats they suspected of smuggling, they burned.

When the war ended in 1865, the economies of Maryland and the other northern states boomed. The demand for oysters immediately picked up to an even greater intensity than before. Schooners again filled the harbors along the Bay with empty baskets dangling from their masts to signal that they were buying, and paddlewheel steamboats resumed their scheduled runs between the Bay villages and the Baltimore docks. Boatyards were besieged by watermen who needed

Brogan carrying oysters to a schooner

new canoes and brogans.

The southerners, however, suffered greatly. Virginia soldiers returning home from the army found that they no longer could make a living on the family farm. Many of them turned to the thriving oyster industry, and some even moved to the islands in the Bay to be nearer the oyster beds. A small group of Virginians settled on an island in the southernmost part of the Smith Island group, and threw up homes that were nothing more than shanties. Even though this tiny island where they lived was inside the boundary of the state of Maryland, they were Virginians and would never associate themselves with any state that had been a part of the hated Union, so they sailed to Accommac County in Virginia to record their deeds and pay their taxes.

Watermen who lived at Somers Cove and Jenkins Creek and Smith Island knew that vast bars of oysters covered a large area of the Tangier Sound from the mouth of the Annemessex River southward across the Virginia boundary line. Since those oysters were in deep water and the watermen could not reach them with tongs, they appealed to the county commissioners to legalize drudging. The commissioners agreed that letting these oysters go to waste was senseless with the demand so great, so they approved an ordinance allowing drudging within Somerset County waters by residents. The only restrictions were that a drudge could not be pulled by any boat driven by a motor, and could not be used in water less than fifteen feet deep. These restrictions were intended to protect the oysters from being depleted, and prevent the tongers who could not work in deep water from being driven off their bars by the bigger drudge boats.

Samuel Lawson and his wife, Ellen, had five children. As did most of the people in Crisfield at that time, they all lived close to the water. The two sons, Bob and Bates, both became watermen like their father. As for the daughters, Mary Ellen married Len Tawes, a schooner captain whose exploits made him famous well beyond Crisfield. The Mariners Museum of Newport News, Virginia, published a book titled *Coasting Captain* containing the journals he wrote about his voyages. Margie married Clarence Diner Sterling, who built up a highly successful marine hardware business one block from the Crisfield docks. Kezzie married Clem Sterling's son. Clem was a prosperous farmer and ship captain who lived on Mariners Road, about a mile from Somers Cove.

Like most of the ship captains on the Eastern Shore, Clem hauled farm produce to Baltimore during the summer and the early fall, then turned to the highly lucrative trade of drudging oysters during the colder months. Clem's ship was much like the ones owned by most of the other oyster drudgers. It was a two masted Bay freighter with huge, square sails hanging from heavy gaffs. It was high sided to give it plenty of room in the hold for freight, but this brought the deck so far above the water that the crew had to struggle unmercifully to haul the drudges aboard. The vast sheets of canvas that stretched between the gaff and the boom gave the ship more than enough power to pull the drudges or drive the heavily loaded hull up the Bay to Baltimore, but they were cumbersome to handle when Clem was trying to stay over the oyster bars.

Clem was making considerably more money drudging oysters than hauling produce, so he questioned why he was sailing a ship that was intended to be a freighter. What he needed was a more maneuverable ship with decks low to the water. It had to be big enough to work in heavy weather, but with a shallow draft so he could slip into the sheltered creeks and coves around the Tangier Sound to harbor overnight, a luxury he could not enjoy with his deep freighter.

Clem discussed his ideas with a ship builder at Somers Cove. They decided that he needed a large log canoe, bigger than any that had ever been built. Clem told him to start it right away.

The builder selected seven huge logs, carved them, and fastened them together like a brogan with long, iron bolts. He decked the entire boat like a schooner so a wave could wash across it without filling it. He put watertight hatches in the center of the deck so Clem could store oysters in the hold, where they would be out of the way and would steady the ship in heavy winds. He built a cabin at the forward end for the crew, and another aft for Clem and the mate. He raked the masts back like a log canoe, and he added a long, tapering bowsprit like a clipper ship. He cut a large hawsehole at each side of the foredeck for the dock lines and the anchor lines to run through. When Clem saw these prominent holes just behind the long needle nose of the bowsprit, he said they made the boat look bugeyed. When someone afterward asked the builder what kind of boat that was, he remembered what Clem told him and replied that it was a bugeye.

Clem's bugeye was as rugged and powerful as he had hoped it would be, yet it was as graceful as any boat on the Bay. Its design had evolved over a span of two hundred fifty years from the combined ingenuity of thousands of Chesapeake canoe builders. With its twin raked masts each flying a triangular sail and its long bowsprit sporting a huge jib, it was so different in appearance from the other large boats on the Bay that it was easily identified. It was also quickly recognized as the perfect oyster drudger. Other canoe builders were soon crawling all over Clem's boat, measuring it and studying its construction.

Oysters were big business in this country, and since most of them were being unloaded at the Baltimore docks, the Baltimore and Ohio Railroad was by far the major carrier. The officers of the Pennsylvania Railroad lusted after this lucrative trade, and decided to gain a part of it. Their plan was to secure a foothold by extending their tracks to some port town along the central Bay, nearer to the oysters than Baltimore. The tiny Eastern Shore Railroad was already working to lay tracks to the village of Somers Cove, the only deep water port near the Tangier Sound, where the richest oyster beds known to man were found. John Crisfield, president of the Eastern Shore Railroad, negotiated the sale, and the Pennsylvania Railroad had its water access.

Gangs of workmen rushed the rails across the flat farm-lands of the Eastern Shore. About a mile from the Somers Cove docks, they ran out of solid ground and bogged down in a marsh. Rather than wait any longer to get into the oyster transportation business, the Pennsylvania Railroad set up a temporary station right there near Mariners Road and began hauling oysters by horse cart from the docks to the waiting box cars while laborers struggled to excavate the soft mud with their shovels and extend the rail bed to the water's edge. When the first train puffed away from Mariners Road in 1866, the fastest route from the oyster beds of the central Chesapeake Bay to the hungry markets in the northeast and midwest was no longer through Baltimore, it was now across the docks at Somers Cove.

With this cheap transportation directly to their customers,

oyster merchants at Somers Cove enjoyed a tremendous advantage over those at Baltimore, for they could bypass the ship captains and purchase their oysters directly from the watermen. They invested in the newly invented steam canneries, which pasteurized the oysters they packed in their cans. Now their oysters would last long enough so they could ship them to cities as far away as Denver. They saw no limit to the number of oysters they could sell, only to the number they could buy and shuck.

Sensing the bonanza there, other oyster merchants, now known as packers, flocked to Somers Cove. They threw up shacks on pilings for shucking oysters. They rolled their shells from the shucking houses and piled them in enormous mounds on the marsh or dumped them overboard. New merchants and tradesmen, such as barrel makers and blacksmiths, leveled the mounds and set up shop, and so the prospering village of Somers Cove spread right out into the Little Annemessex River on a firm base of sun bleached oyster shells.

Watermen on the Eastern Shore, who in the past had been able to earn just enough money to keep body, soul, and boat together, now were caught up in a frenzy over oysters. They knew they could get a good price for them at the Somers Cove docks. Even a waterman who owned a smaller boat, as Samuel Lawson did, could live as well as his cousins who had moved to the city for employment. Samuel hired a young man from the neighborhood to go along with him as a crewman. They spent every decent day except Sunday tonging, sold their catch in the late afternoon, and divided the money right then. Samuel took one third for himself and one third for the boat. Then he gave the other third to the crewman. After settling up, they sailed for their anchorage at Jenkins Creek and walked home to spend the night.

Drudgers, however, endured an entirely different way of life. Their boats needed bigger crews, eight to ten men to crank the winches that pulled the heavy, oyster clogged drudges onto the decks. The work was hard, more than a human should have to bear, so the local men who could find any other work would not take such a job. The drudge boat captains were therefore obliged to hire any man they could get, and often signed on drifters and fugitives.

These drudge boat crews spent their days dragging up oysters off the bottom of the Tangier and Pocomoke Sounds. They dumped them in the hold without making any attempt to cull the smaller oysters from the usable ones, and sailed for Somers Cove before dark with so many aboard that their decks were often awash. They unloaded at the dock and, since they were paid by the season rather than by the day, they collected a small advance from the captain. They then hurried to one of the many saloons that now crowded the waterfront and spent their handful of cash in a night of wild revelry. They drank themselves into a stupor at the saloons, brawled in the streets, returned to their drudge boats reeling and bloody, and woke up at dawn over the oyster rocks.

The townspeople accepted the riotous behavior of the crews for only one reason. They brought in lots of oysters, and the town's prosperity depended on that. Packers built huge Victorian houses with slate roofs and turrets and wrap around porches. Drudge boat owners made enough money in a single winter season to live well all the rest of the year, and often had plenty left over to add another new boat to their fleet.

Somers Cove was no longer a peaceful little village. It had become a bustling seaport filled with speculating businessmen, transient laborers, and rugged oystermen. Violence was so commonplace around the docks that it threatened the entire community. In an attempt to control the rampant lawlessness, the townspeople elected to incorporate into a city. They named it Crisfield, in honor of John Crisfield, president of the Eastern Shore Railroad, who had been so instrumental in bringing them prosperity.

In 1872, just six years after the railroad tracks reached Mariners Road and a full two years before they were carried to the water's edge, the town of Crisfield surpassed mighty Baltimore to become the leading oyster port in the world. By the mid 1880s, the Chesapeake Bay was the world's most productive oyster fishing grounds. Maryland watermen alone were producing thirty-nine percent of the oysters caught in the United States, and more than all the other countries in the world combined. The Maryland oyster catch made up seventeen percent of the total value of all the combined fisheries in the United States. The federal government commissioned a study of this important industry in the late 1890s. The results, published in 1900, declared Crisfield the *SEAFOOD CAPITAL OF THE WORLD*.

The rapid transportation straight from the docks to the big cities also gave Crisfield a market for the more perishable seafood that had previously been of no commercial value. Watermen who had depended on the winter oyster season for most of their income now kept the packers busy during the warmer months with boat loads of fish and crabs. Money poured into town all year round. In 1904, the Bureau of Fisheries declared Crisfield the greatest crab shipping point in the United States.

In less than forty years, the village that was merely a tiny cluster of shanties beside Somers Cove had grown to become the queen of the Chesapeake, and was the second most populous city in the state of Maryland. It even had its own customs house, and by 1910 more sailboats were registered there than at any other port in the United States.

     When Virginia and I visited the Mariners Museum in Newport News several months earlier, I purchased a book titled *Chesapeake Bay Log Canoes and Bugeyes*. I remembered a table in the back that listed all the bugeyes built and registered in the United States customs house. Any boat over forty feet long had to be registered, so that would include most of the bugeyes.

     I took the book from its place on the top shelf of my library and sat down beside my reading lamp. I turned to the table in the back and found that it listed the boat names in alphabetic order. For each boat, the registration number, the place where it was built, the date registered, the size of the boat, and the name of the builder were included. I skimmed the pages of this table. Crisfield frequently appeared as the place where a boat was built. So did places with names such as Monie, St. Peter, Inverness, and Fishing Island. Most people would not know where these were, because they did not appear on any road maps, but I remembered hearing about them. Some were small communities near Crisfield, others were merely shallow harbors along the Tangier Sound whose names showed up only on the Bay's nautical charts.

     I was curious as to how many of the boats were built near Crisfield, so I counted them. Of the five hundred ninety-six bugeyes listed on the chart, I found two hundred eighty-three that were built in or very near to Crisfield. That was an amazing forty-seven percent of all the bugeyes registered. Considering that a lot of records were lost when the Crisfield customs house burned in 1881, over half of the bugeyes could have easily been built there.

I examined the table again, this time looking at the names of the men who built these distinctive boats that were the mainstay of the Chesapeake oyster fleet during the glory days of the industry. One name caught my eye. It was T. Byrd of Crisfield, who built a bugeye named the *George Todd* in the year 1883. I skimmed to the end of the table. This was the only boat credited to him. I went back to my library and pulled out my genealogy records of Crisfield. The only T. Byrd I could find any mention of at this time was Thomas Byrd, a sail maker. He married Suzie Mariner, and built a house on the land her father gave to them near Jenkins Creek. Hon and I were both born in that house. Thomas Byrd was our great grandfather.

Chapter 5
A Time of Exploiting

Jamie worked with Hon on the crabbing boat six weeks before he returned to college for the second part of the summer session. He assured us that he urgently needed the class he was going to take, but I didn't remember him mentioning it at the beginning of the summer. Hon said he and Jamie had both benefited a lot from the experience. Jamie had a natural feel for the water and had been a big help on the boat. And Hon was certain that he returned to school with a new passion for learning.

On our next visit to see Floyd and Margaret, Hon stopped by the house shortly after dark and invited me to go crabbing in the morning. I asked him if anyone else would be going along, because I knew that thirty years in an office had softened me too much for a full day of pulling in pots. He said his regular crewman was off, but his son, Mike, was taking a few days vacation from his job as an aircraft mechanic to help out. I told him if that was the case, I would be happy to go. Since Hon shoved off from the shanty wharf at five, I would have to get up a little after four. I looked at my watch and saw that was less than eight hours away, so I said good night to Virginia and Margaret and Floyd, and I trudged up the stairs.

By four-thirty, I had dressed in my only pair of blue jeans, slipped on a light jacket to guard against the cool morning breeze blowing across the water, finished a breakfast of cereal and toast, and was walking down the road toward Jenkins Creek. The wind was light from the southwest, which was good, but ominous clouds blotted out the stars. A faint grayness in the eastern sky hinted at the approach of a dawn. I thought back to when I was a teenager and walked this road at night in the pitch like darkness by feeling my way along the edge with my bare feet. I wondered how many other conveniences of modern urban living besides street lights I was taking for granted and could no longer imagine being without.

The only house on the road that showed a light was Hon's. I passed by as silently as I could to avoid arousing his dogs and waking the neighborhood. I thought back to when every kitchen window would have shown a glimmer at this time of morning, because the people who lived along this road then were all watermen and would be out on their boats by dawn. But now, most of them didn't have to get up so early because they worked in town, if they had any work at all.

I was the first one to reach the creek that morning. I walked down the long wharf and around to the south side of the shanty where Hon kept his boat. Here, I knew I could find a bench or some crates to sit on while I waited for him to show up. I didn't have to wait long. I soon heard his old pickup rattle to a stop beside the wharf, and within a couple of minutes he had turned on the light and flung open the door beside me.

"You're up early," he said.

"Didn't want to miss the boat," I replied as I blinked to shut out the glaring light.

"Gotta fish out the soft crabs. Then we'll be ready to go."

He picked up his short handled dip net and walked over to the big, low sided tanks stacked two high against the back wall of the building. A stream of salt water poured into each tank from a white plastic pipe suspended above it. A drain within the tank kept the water depth at about five inches, plenty for the mat of green shelled crabs that covered the bottom. He dipped a bucket of water from the nearest tank and set it on a ledge. He then scooped up half a dozen soft, freshly molted crabs with his net and gently dropped them into the bucket.

"Howdy!"

John, a waterman who leased a space at the shanty for his boat, stepped through the door. Behind him trailed his mate, loaded down with as many buckets and baskets as he could possibly carry.

"Go put them in the boat," John instructed him. "I have some business here with Hon."

"Must be pay day," Hon said as he wiped his hands on his pants and called Mike from the packing room to finish dipping out the soft crabs.

John pulled a folded piece of paper from his shirt pocket and handed it to Hon. "Here's the statement for the crabs I bought last week," he said as he handed it to Hon. "And here's the money to pay for 'em."

He reached into his pants pocket and pulled out a thick wad of bills with a rubber band around them.

"Count that to make sure it's right," he told Hon as he handed it to him.

"I know it's right," Hon said, cramming the note and the wad of bills into the right front pocket of his pants.

I chuckled to myself at Hon's record keeping system. His right pocket was for business, and his left pocket was for personal spending money. At the end of the day, he emptied his right pocket onto the kitchen table. Any scraps of paper regarding financial transactions went into a coffee can, any money he needed to cover personal expenses went into his left pocket and any that was left over went into the bank. A simple system, and accurate, too. At the end of a crabbing season, he added up all the income statements in the can, subtracted all the expenses, and he knew exactly how much profit he had made, if any. As for taking the money without counting it, Hon would not do that with everyone. But John was honest to the core, and every week Hon showed his faith in his friend's integrity with this simple act.

Crabbers don't allow much time for socializing in the morning, so John's stay at the shanty was brief. His motor rumbled to life, his mate threw the lines off, and John eased his big forty-six footer out into the channel. Hon watched until he was clear, then turned to packing the soft crabs into waterproof cardboard trays that held about four dozen each.

"John runs a truck full of crabs up to Philadelphia after work every day," Hon said as he laid the dripping crabs neatly into the tray. "He gets a better price there than we can get in Crisfield, so I send as many by him as I can. It's a long trip after a full day's work. I don't know if he'll be able to keep it up."

Hon stacked the trays on one another and lifted them from his packing bench.

"Open the cooler doors for me," he said. "I'll put these inside and we'll be ready to go."

The big V8 Chrysler sputtered, belched a blast of black smoke from the twin exhausts above our heads, and roared to life. Mike cast the lines loose and disappeared into the forward cabin before Hon thought of something else for him to do. One of the benefits of being a crewman is you can stay up at night and sleep during the run to the pots. Hon pulled the throttle back to a rumbling idle, slipped the gearshift lever into forward, and turned the big boat's bow toward the channel. Ten thousand pounds of carefully crafted Eastern Shore oak and yellow pine slipped slowly through the water, leaving hardly a ripple behind.

As soon as he passed the last shanty and no longer had to

worry about his wake bouncing boats against a wharf, Hon pressed in the throttle. I staggered from the sudden acceleration, then scrambled forward, as far away from the deafening motor as possible. Sheets of spray showered out from each side as the boat punched its way through the waves. We would cruise at this speed until we reached the Pocomoke Sound, about twenty minutes away.

Conversation was now out of the question, so I began to study my surroundings. The boat was a heavily built, forty-two foot roundstern. The forward deck was plentifully large enough for a man to stand on while working with the dock lines or pulling an anchor. In the middle of that deck was a huge post that extended all the way down to the keel, where it was solidly bolted. That post, aptly named the Samson post, to me symbolized the construction of the Chesapeake work boat. I never heard of a Samson post ever breaking, not under any conditions, no matter how many lines were tied to it, no matter how hard the wind blew. These watermen who worked the Bay trusted their lives to their boats daily, and would not tolerate flimsy construction just to save a few dollars.

Aft of the forward deck stood the cabin, where Mike was now stretched out asleep on a bunk. I was standing just behind that cabin, in the open hold of the boat where the crew worked and the catch would be stored. A sturdy awning covered this spacious hold to ward off the burning summer sun. Taking up a large portion of the aftermost part of the hold was a huge box that held the roaring Chrysler, and also served as a workbench. The engine controls were on the back of the box, convenient to Hon's left hand as he stood by the steering wheel.

We rounded the beacon that marked the entrance to Broad Creek, a dredged channel that cut through the marsh to the Pocomoke Sound where Hon had his pots. Our rolling wake washed against the shore on each side of the channel, ruffling the sharp bladed marsh grass and spraying foam into the wild cherry trees that clung by their exposed network of roots to the eroding bank.

As we rounded a tree covered bend, the creek widened and opened to the Pocomoke Sound. A slight swell rose to meet us, broke against our charging boat, and drenched Hon with spray as he stood at the wheel. He slowed the engine down a bit so we could stay dry, at least until we began pulling the crab pots. I glanced over our starboard side, and far to the west I could see Watkins Point. Several hazy patches of low marsh stretched out across the water from there, and on one of them I could barely make out a building that I knew to be a hunting lodge.

"Foxes Island," Hon shouted over the roar of the motor. "Most of it has washed away since the last time you were there."

Hon dropped the motor back to idle and shifted into neutral. I looked to the east, toward the rising sun, and to my amazement the waves were littered with bobbing corks of all colors. About ten boats were already working there. I wondered how they managed to maneuver between the buoys without constantly running over them.

"The orange ones are ours," Hon said. "Orange cork with a white paddle sticking up."

Mike dragged out of the cabin, pulled on a pair of thick rubber gloves, sleepily staggered across the rolling boat, and grabbed ahold the steering wheel. Hon pulled the strap of a black rubber apron over his head and set up his culling bench next to the engine box. He dropped a couple of baskets on the floor beside him, shoved his hands into his thick gloves, and handed me a pole with a hook at the end.

"Here, Glenn. You hook 'em, pull the buoy in, and pass it to Mike. He'll wrap the line around the winder and jerk the pot to the surface. Then he'll set it on the engine box. You turn it right side up facing me and unhook the lid. I'll dump it and put it on the end of the bench. Then you close the lid and get it ready to throw. Just before you hook the next pot, throw the one you have. And make sure you get it far enough away from the boat so we don't run over the line."

I couldn't believe he had so carefully thought out his routine. I had imagined he would just motor up to a pot, pull it and shake the crabs from it, and throw it back.

He must have sensed my astonishment.

"We have six strings of pots to fish this mornin', three hundred eighty in all, so we need to be organized," he said.

I calculated that we would have to average about sixty pots an hour to finish by noon. But we would also be spending time moving from one string of pots to another. That meant we would be picking them up, shaking out the crabs, and tossing them back at better than one per minute.

Mike eased up to the first buoy. Just as I reached over with the hook he shifted into reverse, stopping the big boat dead in the water. A wave lifted the buoy up beside me and I slashed at it with the hook.

I missed!

"Under it," Hon shouted. "Get your hook under it!"

I leaned out as far as I could and slashed again, this time just under the bobbing cork, and snagged the line. I tugged at it, but nothing moved. I set my feet and tugged again, as hard as I could. This time I felt the pot break loose from the bottom. I pulled the pole in, hand over hand, until I could grab the dripping line. Then I tugged to get some slack in it so I could pass the cork to Mike.

81

I turned and looked at Hon. He was shaking his head in disgust.

"You gotta move a lot faster than that, or we won't be finished by this time tomorrow. The wind is blowin' us away from the pots, so Mike has to put the boat as close as possible, but you'll only get one chance. Don't miss it, 'cause we'll take four times as long whenever we have to circle back. And you gotta whip that hook over to Mike as soon as you snag the line. If we take too long to get a pot out of the water, the boat drifts off course, like it did this time, and that slows us down."

Hon had plenty of time to instruct me as Mike struggled to bring the bow of the boat back in line with the string of orange buoys. He took the pot from the top of the engine box, unhooked it, shook out most of the crabs, and set it on the bench beside me.

"That's the bait," he said as he nodded toward the two large male crabs still clinging to the inside of the pot.

Watermen are avid marine biologists, not out of curiosity but out of necessity. They study the life cycles of the Bay creatures, and adapt their fishing methods to take advantage of each new discovery. Many years ago, they learned that the female crabs migrate up from the mouth of the Bay in hordes as the water warms each spring. They begin their journey as juveniles, only a couple of inches across the shell. As they outgrow their protective armor, the hard shell splits across the back and the crab instinctively searches for a place to hide. It knows that when it wiggles free from the shell it will be helpless and completely vulnerable to any passing fish looking for a meal. If the crab survives for a few hours, it absorbs enough minerals and nutrients from the water to harden the shell again and it reverts to its familiar, nasty nature.

The young crab grows by about one third each time it

sheds. As it increases in size, it has a harder time finding a place to hide. At about five inches in length, the female reaches maturity and seeks the protective embrace of an obliging male when she is ready to shed. So watermen, whenever they sense an abundance of females, leave a few large males in their pots and let the natural biological process take its course.

As we approached the next pot I threw the first one, grabbed my hook, reached out, and snagged the line under the passing buoy. I set my feet and whipped the buoy back toward Mike. He grabbed the line, wrapped it around the drum of the winder, and the pot popped to the surface.

"That's good," Hon said as he nodded approvingly.

We ran down that string of pots in less than an hour. I eagerly peered into each one as it broke the surface, for I never knew what it would hold. A dozen consecutive pots might hold twenty crabs or more, then the next two could be practically empty. Sometimes a fish would be trapped inside, but more often a sea nettle would be tangled in the wire mesh. Sea nettles are messy. They are a kind of jelly fish with long, stinging tentacles. They ooze through the mesh and plop onto the floor of the boat as slippery gobs. Worse yet is when a flapping flounder shares a pot with a sea nettle, spattering the stinging tentacles all over the boat and in everybody's face and eyes.

As we motored the short distance to the next string of pots, Hon lifted the lid off his basket of peeler crabs and glanced inside.

"The catch is improvin' these past few days," he said. "I'll soon be able to meet my bank payment if this holds up."

At this point, I was more concerned about my back holding up. I had already figured out that I would not be able to pull all three hundred eighty pots. If I made it to a hundred, I would be lucky. Meanwhile, Hon looked as fresh as if his day had just begun. I guess it had, for three hundred thirty of his orange buoys remained in the water ahead of us.

"I had to borrow right heavy to fit out this year," he said, "but we didn't catch many crabs the first month, like we usually do. So when my banker called last week to remind me the note was due, I told him I didn't have the money to pay it. He asked me what I was going to do about it. I told him the only thing I could think of was to hang up."

Tired as I was, I had to laugh. I couldn't imagine telling my banker that. But watermen have always been the most independent people I ever met. Even though times were now tough, Hon still retained that attitude. I hoped he would never have to change.

Mike lined up on the string of buoys and aimed for the first one. This time we were headed in the opposite direction, into the wind. As we approached the buoy, I was confident it would be well beyond my reach.

"Better get closer to it," I shouted.

"Get ready," Mike shouted back. "With the wind blowin' this way, we'll drift right on top of it."

"Don't miss one now," Hon added. "If you do, the buoy will go under the boat. Then the line wraps around the turnin' propeller shaft and winds the pot up and twists it around the propeller."

"That's when somebody goes swimmin'," Mike added with a frown.

I was afraid to ask who would go swimming, but I figured it would be the one at fault. I needed no more warning.

The work was much easier going into the wind. With the waves driving us toward the pots, the lines had more slack and were easier to pull. Maybe I would be able to hold out for a couple of hours if we didn't have to fish another string running with the wind.

I had my eye on a buoy bobbing about a boat length ahead when I heard a muffled 'clunk' behind me. As I turned to see what caused the noise, Mike shut off the motor. Without saying a word he walked forward to the cabin, reached inside, and pulled out an anchor. He climbed up to the foredeck, tossed the anchor over the side, and tied the line to the Samson post. He then walked back to the stern, kicked off his shoes, and jumped overboard, feet first. He surfaced right beside the boat, reached up, and grabbed the rail. Hon handed a knife down to him, then he disappeared under the stern.

After about a minute, he came up.

"It's really wrapped tight," he sputtered to Hon.

Up until then, neither of them had uttered a word.

"Try again," Hon told him. "I sure can't afford to get towed to Crisfield and hauled out to cut it off."

Mike disappeared again. He came up with a tangled line in his hand and a yellow cork bobbing behind him.

"It's somebody else's pot," he sputtered. "I never saw it. It must have gotten out of their line."

Encouraged by this small victory, Mike submerged again. But when he came up this time, he grabbed ahold the stern and wearily hung on.

"Gotta rest before I go down again," he gasped.

Hon pulled a rusty set of tin shears from his tool box, kicked off his boots, and jumped overboard with a gigantic splash. When he surfaced, he took a deep breath and disappeared under the stern. I could feel the boat shaking under me as he wrestled with the twisted pot. He came up, hung onto the stern until he caught his breath, then went down again. The boat shook a couple more times, then he burst to the surface. He tossed a mangled ball of wire and steel rods up onto the deck. Mike and I reached down, grabbed his belt, and struggled to haul him aboard.

While Hon sat panting on the stern, Mike went forward to the cabin, pulled off his wet jeans, and put on his spare pants. He ran a line from the cabin to the back part of the awning, then fastened his pants to it with a couple of clothespins so they could dry. After Hon had rested a few minutes, he changed and hung his dripping pants beside Mike's jeans.

We were soon moving again, but the wind had shifted and was now blowing strongly from the northwest. The waves were splashing into my face as I leaned over to hook the buoys, and pulling the pots was much harder than it had been before we tangled with the stray.

"Looks like the weather is turnin' for the worse," Hon observed. "Hope we can finish before it gets too bad."

The wind picked up by the minute. We pulled a couple more pots, and then I heard Mike yell, "Quick, hand me the hook!"

He grabbed the hook from my hand, dashed to the other side of the boat, and began stabbing into the water. His jeans had blown off the line. Hon ran back to the controls and maneuvered the boat in the direction Mike last saw his jeans. Then Hon's pants flapped loose from the line and sailed over the stern.

He threw the boat into reverse and bellowed at Mike, "Get my pants!"

Mike yelled back, "What about mine?"

"Yours don't have fifteen hundred dollars in the pocket!"

Mike dropped the hook, raced to the stern and leaped for Hon's sinking pants. I grabbed the hook and jumped up on the deck to help. But I landed squarely atop a jelly fish. Both feet shot out from under me and I plunged head first into the water.

When I came up, I saw that Mike had saved Hon's pants. He handed them up, and Hon immediately thrust his hand into the right front pocket.

"Empty," he moaned. "Did you see any money floatin' in the water?"

"No," Mike replied as he hung onto the side of the boat. "Maybe you dropped it when you changed your pants."

Hon ducked into the cabin and popped right back out, triumphantly waving the roll of bills. With the emergency now ended, he helped the two of us scramble back into the boat. As Mike and I stood shivering in the wind and wringing the water from our clothes, Hon shifted into forward and turned the boat toward Broad Creek.

"Are you going to fish any more pots?" I asked.

"No," he replied. "The wind's a blowin' so strong we'll beat 'em to pieces against the side of the boat. And besides that, this has already been my worse day of the year and we haven't picked up a hundred pots yet."

Then he mumbled something else I couldn't quite make out, something about knowing better than to invite a Jonah aboard again.

After supper that night, Hon dropped by the house.

"I won't be going with you tomorrow," I said.

"That's right," he replied.

I woke up before day break the next morning, dressed, ate a bowl of cereal, and slipped out the back door. Since I wasn't going crabbing there was no need to walk to the creek, so I set out for Crisfield. I walked until I reached the old railroad docks that ended at the river. Then I turned around and watched the town stir to life. From the east, a string of headlights flowed toward me along Maryland Avenue. Those would be the cars and trucks of the men who opened the crab picking houses. To the west, red and green glows danced across the water, marking the crabbing boats headed out toward the Pocomoke Sound.

I looked south, facing the wind, to where Hammock Point juts out into the river. Here, a lone house glistened in the first rays of the morning sun. This point of land and this house, to me, were symbols of the past glory of Crisfield.

The house was built by a man named Albert LaVallette. He arrived in town with a dream, he wanted to build a seafood empire. And he had a plan for fulfilling that dream, a plan that centered on a common little salt water turtle, the diamondback terrapin.

The terrapin was so abundant during the years before the Civil War that plantation owners turned to it as a cheap source of food for their slaves. The Maryland legislature passed a law that forbade feeding terrapin to slaves more than two meals a week. This law was for the benefit of the slaves, not the terrapin, for it was not a tasty dish. When slavery ended, the terrapin returned to obscurity, and seemed destined to remain hidden away in the marshes.

But Albert, during a trip to the Caribbean islands, had come upon a recipe that transformed the terrapin into a savory delicacy. When he returned from this trip, he began to search for a good place to start his business. He knew that the waters and marshes of the central Chesapeake were alive with terrapin, and that Crisfield was the most prominent seafood town in this area. The crab processing houses there were producing tremendous piles of foul smelling crab shells and fat. This waste was a nuisance to the crab house owners, but Albert knew that it would be an ideal food to fatten terrapin while they were penned up waiting to be sent to the markets in the cities.

A speedy transportation system was also important to Albert. Crisfield was the only town near the marshes of the central Bay that had a railroad. It was also a major Chesapeake port, with regular steamship service from there to Baltimore and to other cities along the Bay.

So Albert packed his bags, purchased a ticket to Crisfield, and climbed aboard a train. When he arrived there, he immediately began his search for a property to purchase. From the docks he could see this point of high land that protruded out into the river right at the mouth of the Crisfield harbor. One old abandoned house sat on the point, but no one had lived in it since William Lawson died.

Albert examined the point and decided it was the perfect place. All the watermen sailing to Crisfield had to pass by it, the water was deep enough for their canoes and crabbing skiffs, the creek beside it would provide a nice shelter for boats, and the marsh behind it could be enclosed with a wire mesh fence to impound the terrapin until he shipped them.

Albert purchased the point, erected a shanty on the edge of the small creek that ran through the property, fenced a section of the marsh, and hired an ancient waterman to live at the shanty, to buy terrapin, and to care for them.

When the crabbers heard that this new city slicker was paying good money for useless terrapin, they were convinced that he was a lunatic. For generations, they had depended heavily upon foraging to put food on their table and would eat just about anything that came from the water or the marshes, but they wouldn't eat terrapin. If this stranger chose to squander his money for worthless things, they figured that they were as entitled to take it as anyone, so they scooped up every terrapin they came across. As they sailed back to Crisfield with their day's catch, they stopped by Hammock Point and sold them to him for a couple of cents apiece, which wasn't much, but was certainly better than nothing at all.

Albert's old waterman spent his mornings sitting in the shade of the porch, cooled by the breeze blowing across the water as he waited for the crabbers to sail up to the wharf with their catch. He counted the terrapins in each basket that a crabber handed up to him, tallied the amount, and dumped them into the enclosed pound. Then, after the last crabber had sailed off, he shoved his own dilapidated sailboat away from the wharf and headed for Crisfield. Here, the day's waste accumulated in growing piles just outside the doors of the crab picking houses. The old waterman shoveled it into baskets, lugged them to the dock and stacked them in his boat. Then, surrounded by this foul smelling cargo and trailing a swarming cloud of flies, he sailed back to Hammock Point. After he dumped the baskets of scrap into the terrapin pound his day's work was over, and he could again retire to the shade of his porch or dangle a line from the end of the wharf to catch a nice rockfish for supper.

A lot of people were happy with this arrangement. The old waterman was happy. He had an easy job and the best breeze in the county. The crabbers were happy because they had another market and a chance to increase their income with very little extra effort. And Albert was happy because he had a dependable source of terrapin and could now go to the next step of his plan.

Albert left the old man in charge of the business and boarded the train to Philadelphia, carrying with him several crates of terrapin. He called on the owners of the most prominent restaurant in the city and told them that he wanted to treat them to a delicacy, the likes of which they had never tasted. They didn't really care to be bothered, but Albert, a resourceful and convincing salesman, persuaded them to allow him use of the kitchen to prepare a dinner for them. He combined his unusual recipe, his personal flair, and his appeal to their egos to make sure they enjoyed the event. When they had finished eating he knew they were impressed, so he put his proposition before them. He offered to license them to use his secret recipe if they would agree to three conditions. They would have to feature his diamondback terrapin at the top of their menu, they would have to make it the most expensive item they served, and they would have to purchase all their terrapin from him.

The owners agreed that the terrapin was delicious, but they did not appreciate anyone dictating terms to them. So they told Albert they did not know if their customers would want to eat reptiles, and they did not care to do business with him.

Albert sweetened his offer. He told them he would sign a contract to give them the exclusive right to his secret recipe and his brand name in the city of Philadelphia, and he would sell the terrapin to them for just a few dollars a dozen. The owners immediately recognized the virtue of reptiles they could buy at such low prices and sell so high, so they reconsidered his proposal.

Albert put the contract in his pocket, picked up his crate with the remaining terrapin, and headed back to the railroad station. He traveled throughout the northern states, called on the most exclusive restaurants, performed before the owners, and made them the same offer.

Within a few weeks, a leading restaurant in every major city in the Northeast had agreed to feature *LaVallette's Diamondback Terrapin* in bold print at the top of the menu. With his contracts in his pocket, Albert returned to Crisfield and busied himself buying terrapin and fattening them as he patiently waited for his plan to bear fruit.

The watermen could see that Albert intended to buy all the terrapin they brought him, so they began to take this part of their business more seriously. In the normal course of a day, a crabber did not encounter many terrapin, for he mostly caught crabs by dragging in the open waters with his sailboat. But he also towed a small skiff, so if the wind died or if the crabs moved closer to the shore where the water was too shallow for the sailboat, he would toss out his anchor, pick up his dip net, and push off in his skiff to search the shallows. Now the watermen crabbed from their skiffs more often, and poled closer to the shore and up into the narrow creeks where they could also find terrapin.

Albert kept purchasing terrapin until they were so thick in his pound that they were crawling all over each other. He fenced a larger section of marsh, and feared that he would be inundated by more of the creatures than he could possible sell.

His worries were without foundation, for in a short time *LaValette's Diamondback Terrapin* became the rage of the epicurean circuit. The few restaurants that were licensed to carry it promoted it heavily, for they found that as well as making a good profit, they gained considerable prestige by being the only establishment in the city where a person could enjoy this delicacy. The fact that it could be found in so few restaurants and that it was so expensive made it all the more appealing, so demand burgeoned. The restaurants clamored for more terrapin.

When Albert's contracts began to expire, his terrapin was firmly established as a gourmet delight. Restaurants that featured it sought to renew their contracts and Albert happily obliged, but with different terms. His new contracts permitted him to offer his terrapins to other restaurants, and the price went up from just a few dollars a dozen to one dollar for each inch of length measured along the bottom shell. Albert's terrapins now cost a hundred dollars a dozen. His turn had come to reap the profits.

With the money that was pouring in, Albert built a lovely villa on Hammock Point so he could closely oversee his operation. His customers soon cleaned out his terrapin pens, so he offered the crabbers higher prices. This increase encouraged them to anchor their sailboats more often and spend more time netting near the marshy banks.

In the big cities, where Albert's customers were all located, the inevitable happened. Other restaurant owners coveted after his recipe but were not willing to pay his price, so they hired the skilled cooks away from their competitors and purchased their terrapin from other suppliers. The dish that had once been enjoyed solely by the wealthy was now within reach of the middle class, who flocked to the restaurants to sample this exquisite fare. Its devotees praised it with a religious fervor. Its reputation grew until it came to symbolize the bountiful delicacies of the Chesapeake, and of the proud Maryland seafood industry. The gentle terrapin was even adopted as the mascot of the University of Maryland, and their athletic teams became known as the Terps.

Buyers scoured Crisfield for terrapin to satisfy the clamoring city restaurants. They offered more money than Albert, so he had to pay more to compete. Terrapin now brought in such a profit for the watermen that some didn't bother catching anything else. They searched the ponds, the marshes, and even the ditches. Every creek near the watermen's homes soon had one or more wire enclosed pounds filled with terrapin awaiting the highest bidder. News of the bonanza spread to other bayside communities. Boatloads of terrapin arrived daily at the Crisfield docks from Smith Island and Tangier, and from far down in Virginia. Every train that left town was packed with crates of live terrapin headed for the city restaurants.

As terrapin became harder to find, the prices increased. Albert's profits faded to where the rewards were no longer worth the effort, so he closed his business and moved back to Philadelphia, leaving behind the empty villa, the terrapin pounds, and the sheds that had served as home and a place of employment for the old waterman.

Faced with overwhelming evidence that the terrapin would soon disappear entirely from the Bay, the Maryland legislature considered a conservation law to protect it. Watermen raised a tumultuous uproar, claiming that any such regulation was a violation of their rights and would cause them irreparable economic harm. The buyers and the restaurant owners joined their voices in the protest, as did those diners whose desire for the dish had been intensified by the scarcity.

In spite of the objections, a regulation to prohibit the catching and selling of terrapin did pass. The buyers returned to the city. The restaurant owners returned beef and lobster to the top of the menu. The watermen also returned to their old ways, oystering in the winter and crabbing in the summer, all the time insisting that laws restricting their catch were unnecessary, for the vast bounties of the Chesapeake were limitless.

I watched from beside the shanty as Hon motored into the

creek. He approached the wharf at a speed much faster than I thought prudent, but then, if he were prudent he would have left the water years ago. When he was about ten feet away he came back hard in reverse, and the bow of the big boat bobbed to a stop right at my feet. He gently maneuvered in against the wharf, then tied the stern as Mike tended the forward line.

"How'd you do?" I asked.

"Decent," he replied. "Caught enough to pay the day's bills, that's all I needed."

He lifted a basket of crabs and slid it onto the wharf. I picked it up to carry it inside. It was not as heavy as I expected. "Does that other basket have any more crabs in it than this?"

"No."

"Crabs aren't very plentiful, are they?"

"Plenty out there, they're just divided among too many crabbers."

I mentioned the terrapin to him, and how they had almost been wiped out by overfishing. I asked if that could now be happening to the crabs.

"Terrapin reproduce slowly," he said. "A terrapin doesn't lay many eggs, so when too many were caught, their natural enemies almost overwhelmed the few that were left. They're just now coming back strong. Crabs are different than terrapin. One crab lays an awful lot of eggs, and they have a better chance of survival nowadays because the fish that used to eat the small ones aren't as plentiful as they used to be."

He climbed onto the wharf, leaving Mike to finish splashing the boat clean with buckets of salty creek water.

"Crabs have a lot going for 'em that terrapin don't," he said. "For one thing, crabs move around. Virginia has set up a sanctuary for 'em, and they migrate from there up to here."

"How do you know the state of Virginia will keep that

sanctuary to supply Maryland with crabs?"

"They can't abandon it without approval from Maryland. Back in the early part of this century, the two states worked out an agreement. The Virginians didn't have as many oysters as we did, so they drudged crabs in the winter. Oysters were becoming scarce in Maryland, and that worried them. They were afraid we'd turn to drudging crabs and flood the market. That would depress the prices and drive a lot of them out of the business. So Virginia agreed that if we wouldn't allow crab drudging in the winter, they would set up a sanctuary to make sure we had plenty in the summer. As long as we don't drudge crabs, they have to keep that sanctuary."

He picked up one basket of crabs and motioned for me to follow him into the shanty with the other.

"That sanctuary arrangement," he said, "shows one reason why we have such a hard time settin' up any regulations that are for the good of the Bay. The two states only agree when somethin' is in it for each of 'em. They don't think about the whole Bay, they're lookin' out for themselves. Unfortunately, the crabs and the fish and the pollution don't know about the boundary."

He set his basket on the edge of one of his wooden tanks and motioned for me to put mine on the floor. He tossed his basket lid into a corner, pulled a crab out, and held it up to the light.

"Pretty good sign," he said as he tossed it into one of the tanks.

"The oysters were almost all caught up, too," I said.

"Not really," he answered. "They became scarce enough so it wasn't economically feasible to keep workin' 'em. Most people quit then, but there were still a lot of oysters scattered about in the Bay. They weren't endangered, but the oyster rocks were damaged badly. Without the proper conditions, oysters don't come back very fast."

He began sorting crabs into the tanks according to the day they would shed. To do this, he pulled each crab from the basket with his gloved hand, spread its swimming fin out and glanced at the spot of color that appears when the new shell begins to separate from the old shell, and then tossed the crab into the appropriate tank.

"Somethin' you need to understand," he said as he pulled a crab from the basket. "There was a lot of money to be made in oysters back then, and that seems to bring out the worst in people, and it also brings out the worst people. You have no idea how lawless the men who worked on the water used to be, especially the drudgers. Yvonne's great grandaddy was a captain on a drudge boat. He slept with a gun in one hand. He tied a line from his other hand to the cabin door so he would know if anyone in his crew tried to sneak in to murder him."

Hon went on to tell me more about the drudgers, what he had read and what had been passed on to him by the old timers who had seen it with their own eyes.

Some of the drudge boats were owned by the captains, but many of them were owned by investors who stayed on shore. The investor generally didn't care what a captain did, so long as he brought back a good profit. And if a captain didn't show enough profit, the owner found someone to take his place. So a captain had plenty of incentive to bring in as many oysters as possible, and to keep down his expenses.

Each captain had to find his own crew. For an average size bugeye, he needed a mate and at least eight crewmen to wind the winches that pulled the drudges up onto the deck. One of these crewmen would also be the cook. A captain tried to take a mate and a cook that he could trust, then he filled out the crew with anybody he could find. The mate and the cook slept in the main cabin with the captain, the remainder of the crew crowded into the smaller forepeak cabin.

When the Civil War ended, many freed slaves heard there was work on the drudge boats, but they soon found that the tyranny on the boats was worse then the tyranny of the cotton fields, so they picked up jobs ashore, usually shucking oysters or unloading boats. As soon as a black boy was old enough to walk, his mother began warning him to never take a job on a drudge boat.

A crewman's life was hard. Drudge boats were designed without any thought for crew comfort. The deck was almost perfectly flat with the two small cabins projecting up only high enough so they didn't fill with water when a man opened the hatch in heavy seas. On blustery days, the wind and the spray and sometimes even the waves swept across the deck while the crew struggled to pull up the drudges as the boat plunged through the white capped swells. On each side of the deck stood a heavy winch with two long handles. Four men would wrestle with each winch to crank the oyster filled drudges toward the moving boat as their teeth still dug through the bar. If a drudge snagged an old wreck or another drudge that someone had lost, the line snatched the winch backward and scattered the men across the deck. If they were lucky and nobody broke an arm or a rib or got thrown overboard, they grabbed the handles again as soon as the captain turned the boat into the wind to stop its forward drive, and then they wrestled with the drudge until they either broke the line or pulled it up. They dumped the drudges onto the deck, then shoveled the oysters down a cargo hatch into the hold to add to the ballast so the boat wouldn't capsize in a gust.

Drudge boats kept going in just about any weather short

of a hurricane. The crew had to learn to keep their feet as they worked on the tossing deck. If a man fell overboard, he sank so quickly the captain often didn't even turn around to try to rescue him.

Cold weather didn't usually stop drudgers unless the Bay froze over. A sudden nor'wester might drop the air temperature well below freezing, but the water temperature changed much more slowly. Every drop of spray that flew over the bow would freeze as soon as it struck the deck, but drudgers kept going until the ice on the boat was so thick they could no longer stand. As soon as they managed to clear it from the deck, they were back drudging again.

If the day ended before the boat was loaded, the captain picked a sheltered cove and anchored for the night. As the crew cleaned up on deck, the cook went below and prepared supper on the wood stove. Then the crew crowded into the warm, main cabin for their meal. They stayed as long as the captain allowed, playing checkers and telling tales while the cook scrubbed the pots and dishes. When the captain drove them out, they fumbled their way through the darkness to their bunks in the forepeak for the cold night's sleep.

If the boat was loaded at day's end, the captain tied up beside a buy boat. The crew shoveled the oysters into tubs and hoisted them over to the other boat as the cook prepared supper. Or, if they were lucky enough to be working close to a good port like Crisfield, they sailed to town and unloaded their oysters there.

Crisfield was the oysterman's favorite port. The captains liked it because of the good prices paid at the packing houses along the docks. The crewmen liked it because when darkness came and the packing houses closed, the dock area became a wild, honky-tonk carnival. Unshaven and unbathed, they flocked into John Blizzard's Burlesque to gawk at the chorus girls he had brought in from Baltimore, and they swarmed around the saloons that lined the back streets near the harbor. Their favorite, on Goodsell's Alley, had a bar at one end of the floor and a boxing ring at the other end. Here, men fought with bare fists until one could no longer stand, or sometimes entire crews climbed into the ring just to see which one could pound the other into retreat.

The fights spilled over into the alley and the streets where the men, no longer restricted by the rules of the ring, battled with knives and broken bottles. The police avoided the dangerous dock area after sundown. As far as they were concerned, the drudgers could do whatever they wanted, as long as they only did it to each other.

There was no more law enforcement on the Bay than in town. When drudging was legalized, the law permitted it only in waters over fifteen feet deep. But when the drudgers cleaned out the oysters there, they began to raid the shallows. In the absence of law, the bigger boat always has the right of way, so the drudgers drove the tongers off their bars. The tongers retaliated by carrying guns to defend their oysters. But the drudgers had guns too, and killed several tongers. The powerless tongers had no choice but to flee, giving up their bars to the bigger, faster, more heavily armed drudge boats.

The tongers appealed to the state of Maryland for protection. The Baltimore newspapers took up their cause, and the state legislators, who were attempting to cover their own corruption with a display of law and order politics, funded the Maryland oyster police. The governor appointed a man named Hunter Davidson as commander. He took the best of the old boats the state provided for his flagship, and led his small band of men out into the Chesapeake to force the unpopular laws on the heavily armed, belligerent drudgers who sailed bigger and faster boats. The oyster police had little success at bringing order to the Bay. The few arrests they made only infuriated the drudgers, who numbered nearly one thousand boats with combined crews of close to ten thousand men.

Davidson anchored his boat in a sheltered cove one evening after patrolling the oyster bars all that day. He assigned watchmen for the night, then went to his compartment and crawled into his bunk. While he and most of the crew were sleeping, a band of drudgers stealthily rowed over to his boat and crept aboard. They knocked the inattentive watchman unconscious, then entered the cabin to murder Davidson. He heard them coming, though, and when they attempted to open his locked compartment, he fired several shots through the door at them. They tried to flee, but he and his aroused crew captured them.

The work of the oyster police was perilous and mostly futile. Attempting an arrest was dangerous, and securing a guilty verdict was even more difficult. The trial would be held in the drudger's home county before a judge who probably was a friend of the family, and the arresting officer was an outsider. To make matters worse, the oyster packers and drudgers were making a lot of money, and their influence in the towns along the Bay was considerable. They contributed heavily to the support of political candidates, and openly bought votes on election day. They opposed any laws offered at the legislature that would strengthen the oyster police, and they attempted to place bureaucrats of their own choice in positions of authority.

Davidson, whose boldness and resoluteness had been responsible for what little success the oyster police enjoyed,

Two drudge boats raiding a tonger bar

resigned in disgust. After his departure, men were placed in leadership positions because of who they knew rather than because of any ability or desire to enforce the law. The newly appointed captains of the police boats refused to confront the drudgers because they knew it was risky, and the police became almost totally ineffective as a deterrent to illegal oystering.

By this time, many of the drudge boat captains had turned to a new source for crewmen. Just before oyster season began, a captain would sail to Baltimore and put in an order with an agent for the number of men he needed. The agent signed up unsuspecting immigrants who had just arrived from Europe and were looking for jobs. Once the immigrants were on board, the captain sailed into the Chesapeake and headed for the oyster bars. He put the immigrants to work at the back breaking winches with the promise that they would share the profits at the end of the season. He sold his oysters to a buy boat, and had any supplies he needed brought out to him. He anchored at night in some cove on one of the marshy islands out in the Bay, and never allowed the crew a chance to go ashore so they could escape. If he needed to go into a port, he locked the crew below in the forward cabin. At the end of the season, he might pay the men something, and he might not. He might just tie up to a dock on the mainland and go down into his cabin for a few minutes, leaving them alone on deck. When he came back up they would be gone, happy to have gotten off the boat even though they had not been paid for the winter's work.

Some captains had another way to dispose of their crew at the end of the season. They would order the immigrants to work on the deck while they ran the boat with the wind. Then they would change course slightly, just enough for the wind to catch the other side of the sail. The sail suddenly whipped across the deck, and the heavy boom swept the crew overboard to drown. This practice they jokingly called 'paying off with the boom.' One place on the Bay was named Bloody Point because so many crews were drowned there.

When the agents could not find enough immigrants to fill the crews, they shanghaied men in the waterfront bars of Baltimore. An agent would pay a bartender to slip a drug in the drink of some unsuspecting customer, and when the unfortunate soul woke up he was out on the Bay. He was forced to work the entire winter in whatever clothes he happened to be wearing when he was brought aboard. If a man died, the captain merely dumped him over the side and ordered another to be brought down on the next buy boat from Baltimore.

As the demand for crewmen increased, the drudgers built prison shanties on pilings in the shallows near the marshy islands where they harbored. Here, they kept their surplus men until they needed them as replacements for their crews.

Tongers like Bob and Bates Lawson, Samuel's sons, found ways to survive when the drudgers drove them from their oyster bars. During decent weather, they tonged on the shallow rocks that were too small for the drudgers to bother. If the weather was calm and the day sunny so they could see individual oysters scattered about on the bottom, they took their small skiffs and their nippers to the Pocomoke Sound. Nippers were miniature tongs set on wooden shafts sixteen feet long. A man could fill his skiff in half a day by nippering, picking up oysters one at a time in the crystal clear water as deep as ten feet.

Bob and Bates sold as many oysters in Crisfield as they had to in order to pay their living expenses. Any oysters they did not have to sell, they shoveled overboard by the wharf alongside their shanty. When the colder weather and the fierce northerly winds came, they no longer took their boats out into the sounds. Instead, they took their guns and paddled their skiffs into the marsh to hunt. Dealers in town bought all the ducks they could kill. Then, when the weather turned really bad, when the Bay froze over so the drudge boats couldn't work anymore and no oysters could be found in Crisfield, Bob and Bates cut through the ice beside their wharf, tonged up their oysters, shucked them, and sold them at a premium price.

The seafood packers hated the tongers. They only bought oysters from them because they needed all they could get to try to satisfy the demands of their customers. The drudgers were bringing in most of the oysters that passed over the docks of Crisfield, so the packers naturally courted them. They used their influence to protect the drudgers as much as possible, and they were beginning to need protection. Immigrant organizations in Baltimore were pressuring the Maryland legislature to pass laws prohibiting slavery on the boats. The oyster industry was strong enough to block such legislation for years, and when it finally passed the oyster police would not enforce the new laws against the friends of their superiors. Even though slavery had been outlawed years ago in this country, it still flourished on the drudge boats.

The drudgers ruled the Bay, and did whatever they pleased. The tongers knew they would get no help from the police, so they banded together for protection. One group captured a drudge boat in the Tangier Sound and burned it, and another group placed a cannon on shore to drive the drudge boats off their bars. The drudgers sneaked ashore during the night, overpowered the watchman, and carried the cannon back to mount on one of their boats. One waterfront town organized a militia to protect the tongers. The drudgers invaded the town, set fire to it, and threatened to burn it down altogether if the militia was ever called into service against them.

The open warfare on the Bay finally forced the oyster police into action. One police boat, while attempting an arrest, was captured by the drudgers. The officers were enslaved for several days, forced to work at the winches, then turned loose in a small boat. Another police boat was attacked but managed to escape. That crew refused to go out on the Bay again.

The state added a new boat, the *Gov. McLane*, to the police fleet, and armed it with a modern cannon. It was big and fast, and its captain was an ex-tonger. This boat became an immediate success at enforcing the laws. The drudgers considered it such a threat that they conspired to destroy it. They attacked it with several drudge boats chained together. But they underestimated the power of the big boat. The *Gov. McLane* rammed two of the attacking drudgers, crushed the boats, and captured the crews.

When the Virginia drudge boats exhausted most of the oysters in their waters, they regularly came over the line to work. The Maryland oystermen complained, so the state sent a police boat to arrest any Virginians they found drudging in Maryland waters. The Virginians then complained that the Maryland police were preventing them from oystering in their own state waters. They argued that since Virginians had been living on the southernmost island in the Smith Island group since the Civil War ended and their deeds were recorded in a Virginia county, then that island was a part of Virginia. They drew a line from the southern shore of the Potomac River across the Bay to the narrow channel just north of the island they claimed, and straight on until it reached the Eastern

Shore. This line divided the town of Crisfield right down the center. According to them, Jenkins Creek, where Bob and Bates harbored their boats and had their homes, was well within Virginia.

Representatives of the two states met in Crisfield to argue about the line while the drudgers and the police fought each other over the oysters in the disputed waters. The two states could not reach an agreement, so the matter was submitted to the federal government. After much haggling, federal arbitrators ruled that since the Virginians had lived on the island for so long without their ownership being challenged, the island belonged to Virginia. They drew a line across the Bay that zagged northward to include the island as a part of Virginia, then southward to where the previous boundary came ashore. Jenkins Creek was still in Maryland, but Virginia gained control over water that the Marylanders considered theirs.

This decision benefited the Virginia drudgers, but it posed a hardship on the Smith Islanders who lived on the Maryland side of the line. When the wind blew from a northerly direction, which it often did during the oyster season, they worked to the sheltered south side of their island. The oysters under this water now belonged to Virginia. The newly defined line also gave Virginia beds of oysters that Jenkins Creek boats had worked when the wind was from the north. Watermen from Smith Island and Jenkins Creek vowed that nobody was going to keep them away from the waters they had worked all their lives.

When the oyster season began the next year, the Smith Islanders sailed their boats to the south side of their island as before. The Virginia police sent a boat out to enforce the line. The Smith Islanders saw it coming and fled back to their harbor, with the police pursuing them all the way. Some of the

Smith Islanders came back to work at the same place the next day, and again the police boat pursued them into their harbor. But this time the Smith Islanders had laid an ambush. They had built a low earthen fort at the entrance to the harbor, and from behind its bank they riddled the police boat with gunfire. Miraculously, none of the police were killed, but they never ventured close to the island again.

The Jenkins Creek watermen who were oystering in the disputed waters were mostly tongers in small boats. They were working so far from their harbor they could not possibly win a battle with the police, so they took a different approach. They moved the buoys that marked the line. They put them where they felt the line should be. Virginia police arrested one of the Marylanders, tried him, and convicted him. He refused to pay the fine, so they locked him up in the Accommac prison.

The Maryland watermen sued in federal court, claiming that the agreement signed during the time of George Washington gave them the right to fish the entire Pocomoke Sound, the body of water that separated the two states on the eastern side of the Bay, just as it gave the Virginians the right to fish the entire Potomac River, which separated the two states on the western side. The court ruled that the agreement only included the narrow Pocomoke River on the eastern side, not the entire Pocomoke Sound. The Maryland watermen, though, refused to accept the ruling, and three generations later, when Hon and I were growing up on Jenkins Creek, the old timers still bitterly defended their right to work across the line.

The Virginia legislature passed a law that legalized the leasing of oyster beds to individuals, and leased out a large bed at a place called Hog Island Bar. The Marylanders considered this bed part of the common territory that could be fished by residents of either state, so they continued to oyster on it. The lease holder hired a gunboat to protect the bar. The first drudge boat caught on the bar was the *Lawson*, owned by a Henry Lawson. The gunboat rammed the *Lawson* and sank it, took the crew off and carried them to Accommac for trial. Henry was enraged. After he paid his fine he returned home, purchased another drudge boat, and armed it heavily. That winter, twelve men were shot to death over Hog Island bar.

The boundary dispute between Maryland and Virginia grew so furious that the two states were practically at war with each other. They directed so much attention to the conflict along the line that no attempts were made in either state to conserve the oysters. With seven thousand boats now working on the Bay, the beds were rapidly depleted.

When the drudgers finally exhausted the oysters in the Tangier Sound, word spread that the Potomac River still had some. The drudgers invaded en masse. The waters of the Potomac became covered with the sails of hundreds of the huge drudgers, dragging up oysters from the first light of dawn until darkness set.

The drudgers expected the same accommodations on the Potomac that they were accustomed to in Crisfield. The townspeople there, however, did not appreciate their drinking and brawling, and the police attempted to arrest them for disturbing the peace. The drudgers assaulted the police, wrecked the towns, and raided the stores and saloons. The residents armed themselves and formed a guard to keep the drudgers from coming ashore again. They were constantly at war with one another until the oysters in the Potomac River gave out, just as they had in the Tangier Sound.

No other place on the Bay had enough oysters to support the huge drudging fleet. Those who were in the business for the quick riches left the Bay. Those who were true watermen had to find some way to cut down their expenses if they were going to get by with the few oysters that remained. They turned to a new type of boat, the skipjack, that was cheaper to build than the bugeye. With its single mast and the newly invented drudge winders powered by gasoline engines, they could now sail with a crew half the size they had needed before.

Many of the bugeye owners cut the graceful bowsprits off their boats and pulled down the masts. They installed motors and turned to carrying freight up and down the Bay, and from the Carolinas through the Chesapeake and Albermarle Canal. The owners of the older boats simply sailed them into coves and abandoned them. Huge graveyards of rotting bugeyes lay in the shallows around Crisfield. The beautiful boat that had once been the mainstay of the Chesapeake oyster industry disappeared from the Bay.

Chapter 6
A Time of Decline

Hon settled back in his recliner with a big glass of iced tea.

"If you want a good first hand account of how drudgers used to live," he said, "go talk to Elmer Riggin. He worked on a drudge boat when he was young. That was after the peak of the oyster catch, but close enough so the times hadn't changed a lot. He's getting into his upper eighties now, but his mind is as sharp as ever. And he loves visitors."

Elmer's house on Sackertown Road was only a short distance across the marshy field behind Hon's, but the paths that knit the little watermen community together when I was a boy were now overgrown, so I had to drive around by the creek to get there. The houses were spaced farther apart on this road. The marsh had taken over most of the land between them, where gardens once grew. A couple of the houses had been purchased by city people who fixed them up and were spending their weekends there, but the others were showing their decades of neglect. Long strips of weathered siding had fallen off, leaving gaps wide enough to reveal the ramshackle rooms inside.

A car was in Elmer's driveway, so I figured he must be home. I parked behind it, stepped out, and looked around to see how much this place had changed. Elmer was an industrious and hardworking man, and I remembered that his house had always impressed me as being neat and clean, as though it had been freshly painted. It was faded and weathered now, but obviously well maintained. The yard, which was not nearly as large as I recalled it from thirty years ago, had been recently mowed.

I knocked on the kitchen door.

"Elmer," I called out.

"Come in, Glenn!"

I opened the door and stepped inside.

"I'm surprised you recognized me," I said.

"I don't forget a neighbor, Glenn, no matter how many years pass. Good to see you. Hope you don't mind me not gettin' up, I can't move around the way I used to. Arthritis has got me all crippled now. Clean off that chair over there. Sit down. Stay a while."

Elmer was hunched over a workbench he had built by the south window of the kitchen, right beside the door. The bench was covered with scraps of wood, small cans of paint, artist's brushes, sandpaper, and a beautiful model of an oystering schooner that must have measured about thirty-six inches from the tip of its bowsprit to its delicate, hand carved stern rail. On the shelf against the back wall of the room a partially completed skipjack sat on its cradle, and to my left two more ships stood under full sets of sail.

"Hope you don't mind the mess, I like to stay busy. I believe I'd go crazy if I didn't have somethin' to do. Glad you came by, I don't see many people nowadays, seems nobody has time to visit, can't sit and talk like they used to, spend a few minutes and then they start fidgetin', gotta get up and go somewhere. Not complainin', mind you, just tellin' you what I see. Don't blame people for not comin' by to see an old man like me. I'm sure I bore 'em to death when I get to talkin'. All I know to talk about is the old times 'cause I can't get around very well any more. But I'm glad you're here. You don't mind if I keep workin', do you? If I stop paintin', I'll have to clean my brush, hardens up right quick, you know."

113

Elmer's hair was snowy white and he was bent over a bit, but other than that, I could not see that he had changed very much. He was still energetic, still filled with an inward happiness that bubbled over on anyone close by. He still talked fast, hurrying to cover all the thoughts that rushed through his quick mind.

"Keep working, Elmer. That's a nice looking boat."

"Thankya. It's the *Edwin and Maud*, one of the boats I remember from when I was a young man. That's what I build, boats I sailed on or ones I saw back in the days when I was sailin'. I build 'em just the way they were built back then, plank by plank, 'cept smaller, of course. Lots of boats been built on this creek. Not just the little crabbin' skipjacks, either. Used to build bugeyes in the woods up at the head of the creek. Oh, that bugeye was a pretty boat. I build my boats from the keel up, cut every frame and plank myself. Make every little cleat and block and deadeye. They're rigged just the way the real ones were, with every sail and every line, just like I remember. Got nothin' but time, but I got plenty of that, so I make every little piece by hand. Look here, you can open the hatch and see down in the cabin."

Elmer slid the tiny hatch cover forward with his forefinger.

"See the bunks down there. That's where the crew slept, in the forepeak. You here for a vacation? My, it's been a long time since I saw you last. You're livin' in North Carolina now, aren't you? I believe that's what Hon told me. I try to keep up best I can."

"I'm just here for the weekend, Elmer. Hon tells me you used to oyster on a drudge boat when you were young. I came by to ask you what that was like."

"Oh my, yes, I oystered on a drudge boat, back about

nineteen twenty or so. The *Dorothy*, she was forty-five feet long, thirteen feet wide, drew three and a half feet of water when she was empty. My first day out, I'll never forget it, we dropped our drudges and started takin' a lick across the bar. The crew ate in shifts. While the drudges were out, half of 'em would go below and gobble down their meal, then they'd come back up to pull the drudges. Soon as we came about and got our drudges out for another lick, the other half would go below to eat. Well now, the captain turned the wheel over to the mate and went below to eat. Boats were so thick on the bar you could hardly see through 'em. The mate was afraid he'd have a collision, so he moved out to the fringe. When the captain came up, he saw we were off the bar. He grabbed up a stick of firewood and hit the mate up side of the head with it. Knocked him right out cold, blood was a runnin' all over the deck. I was sure he had killed him. I was ready to go home right then, but there wasn't any way to get off the boat.

"They were rough men, and impatient. I've never seen such impatient men. All they could think about was catchin' oysters. One captain out there had five boats, one fast schooner and the rest were bugeyes and skipjacks. He skippered the schooner. All five boats would drudge until they caught enough oysters to fill the schooner. Then he'd sail for Baltimore to sell 'em, that was where the best price was paid, but you couldn't afford to sail up there every time you caught a boat load. You normally just sold to buy boats that ran the oysters to Crisfield every day, but that schooner held so many he could make a good profit sailin' it to Baltimore when he loaded it. Well, he was drudgin' the schooner one day along with his other four boats, and one of the other skippers kept gettin' in his way. The oyster rocks were so crowded back then, they were just covered with boats. My, that was a pretty

115

sight, to see all those boats under full sail on a nice breezy day, so close together the crews could talk to each other. Well now, this other boat kept gettin' in his way, and it made him so mad he ran right over her. Ran over his own boat, mind you, 'cause it was in his way. Busted her open like a ripe watermelon, sank right there, load of oysters and all. Sank right on the middle of the bar. Ha! Been in everybody's way ever since. Been many a drudge hang up on her.

"A drudge boat our size carried five men, captain, mate, cook, and two crew. The captain, mate, and cook slept in the cabin, the crew slept in the forepeak. Bigger boats had a crew of three or four in the forepeak. I was the cook on our boat. The cook worked with the crew, but he didn't have to clean up the boat at the end of the day. Instead, he had to get up an hour before anybody else to start breakfast. The drudges went over the side at the first light of dawn, so I was up mighty early.

"One good thing about being cook, I got to pick the food we would eat. I cooked a bread pone every night for supper, had fish and beans with it. For variety, I'd cook white beans one night, red beans the next, and lima beans the night after that. Then I'd start over again with the white beans. And if we harbored where I could get to a marsh, I'd take my gun and go kill a few ducks for supper while the crew was cleanin' up. One time, we got froze up while we were harborin' in a cove behind a marshy island, looked out in the mornin' and the Bay was a solid sheet of ice. We had to stay there so long that all we had left to eat was oysters and duck. We got down to our last bucket of coal before the ice broke up so we could make our way ashore.

"We stayed out from the first week of November 'til Christmas Eve before we got to come home the first time. A boat would come out from Crisfield every day to buy the oysters we'd caught, so we only went ashore about once a week to get food and to walk on land for a change. Soon as we had grubbed up, back out we went. We didn't have a radio, so we tried to get a weather report whenever we went ashore. The Crisfield customs house had a flag system, one red flag on the pole for a warnin', two flags for a gale, and three for a hurricane. We were rarely close enough to see the flags, and if they were up nobody was fool enough to come out, so we never got a warnin'.

"Drudgin' was hard work, Glenn, but I enjoyed it. Dangerous work, too. One January day I remember, it was just like summer, warm and sunny, the crew was workin' in their shirt sleeves, it was that warm. Nearly calm, we had the sail stretched out, all we could raise, but we could only pull one drudge, and pitifully slow at that. We were just lazin' around on the deck when the captain called us to reef the foresail. At first, we thought he was jokin', but then he began to curse and yell for us to hurry. He had us reef that foresail down to the last points and take down the jib. Just about the time we were finished shortenin' sail, I looked to the nor'west and all I could see was white water and spray a flyin'. We hauled up the drudge and the captain turned the boat to run with the wind, but when that gale hit us it drove the bow under, right under, mind you, with the sail reefed down to the last points. The water came surgin' over her and the only thing I could do was hang on for dear life. Washed every oyster overboard, cleaned the deck. When the bow came up, she took off, gained a good headway and never plunged under again.

"But that wasn't the roughest trip. One day a storm hit us and we took down every scrap of sail. Didn't have any motor, mind you, took down every scrap of sail and ran before the wind with just our bare poles. We turned in behind an island to hole up until the blow let up some. Another boat, much bigger than ours, came by us. I recognized it as the one my brother-in-law crewed on. It was runnin' bare poles too, but it didn't turn up behind the island like we had. Instead, it headed across the Tangier Sound for Crisfield. When it got out in the middle of the sound, out of our sight, the wind caught behind the boom. Now, it didn't have a scrap of sail up, mind you, none at all, but the wind was blowin' so strong it swept that boom across her deck and slung my brother-in-law overboard. The captain was afraid to try to turn her around, so he ordered the crew to put the little boat overboard. How they got it over without swampin' it, I'll never figure out. One man climbed in the boat and tried to row back against the wind to pick up my brother-in-law, but he couldn't get back in time. The captain kept runnin', didn't even try to pick up the small boat, that's how bad the wind was. When he got to Crisfield, he reported two men drowned. The man in the small boat somehow managed to scud all the way across the sound and get behind an island where he was picked up by another boat, but my brother-in-law was lost. That captain never went drudgin' again, and neither did I. I know I'm borin' you to death, Glenn. I appreciate the company, though. Don't let me run you off with all my jabberin'."

I assured Elmer he wasn't boring me at all. I asked him when he began working on the water. He swished his brush around in a small can of solvent and laid it on the table to dry.

"I just skip around from one thing to another, eventually I finish a boat. I'll paint a while on one, then I'll carve a while and then I'll plank a while on another."

He picked up his knife and began carving the spokes of a miniature steering wheel.

"I began goin' on a crabbin' boat when I was eight years

old, just to steer and to clean up. When I was thirteen, we were havin' such a bad year that a waterman would only catch four or five crabs a day. A man couldn't live on that little money, so most everybody quit the water and went lookin' for a job ashore. The man I was workin' with sailed all the way to Kedges Straits, three hours each way, and caught one crab that day. He left the next mornin' to look for a payin' job. Stouty owned the boat we were crabbin' on, and he let me take it by myself that day. I caught twenty-five crabs, most of any man on the creek. Oh, I felt mighty big about that. Next day I caught about that many again, and I was proud as could be, sailin' up to the shanty with my crabs in the basket to show off. Trouble is, I forgot to put my centerboard down, and when you tried to turn one of those skipjacks without puttin' the board down, it just slid sideways through the water. I bounced off the shanty wharf, snagged the sail on a stake, and ripped it from the boom clear up to the peak.

"Oh, my, I was scared to death. I was sure Stouty would never let me in one of his boats again, but he just told me to pull the sail down and carry it to the sailmaker at the head of the creek. That sail was sixty yards of heavy canvas. I had to get somebody to help me put it on my back, but I carried it every step of the way. Next mornin' I hauled it back to the creek and put it back on the mast, never even missed a day of crabbin'. In a couple of weeks, the crabs came back. Stouty let me keep the boat because I had stuck with him and had caught crabs when the others quit.

"That was back before anyone had an engine in a crabbin' boat. We pulled two scrapes with a boat, three if the boat was big enough. We tied one to a cleat at about amidship so it would drag down beside the boat, the other we tied off the stern cleat on the opposite side of the boat so it would stay clear of the first. If we pulled a third, we rigged a pole off the side of the boat to keep it away from the other two.

"Must have been more than twenty boat builders on the creek back then, built bateaus and skipjacks and crabbin' skiffs. Back before my time they built canoes and brogans and bugeyes. Those were heavy boats, had to be built right next to the water. Carved boats they were, you know, not built with frames and planks like bateaus and skipjacks.

"When I was young, a bateau had two sails and a skipjack had one. Then the distinction got to be blurred. If a man said that the boat he built was a skipjack, then it was a skipjack, whether it had one sail or two. One man might say he built a bateau and another say he built a skipjack, but sometimes I couldn't see any difference.

"When I was a young man, I had a skipjack for crabbin'. Crabs move around, you know. One day they'd be in the Pocomoke Sound, next day they'd be gone. I've chased after crabs as far away as Hollands Straits, a four hour sail from the creek. Took one full hour to sail across the Tangier Sound, and that could get mighty rough. One day I was sailin' home in company with another crabber and a squall came up. We each took down our sails and scudded across the sound under bare poles. The waves were so high I'd lose sight of him when we went down in the troughs, couldn't even see the top of his mast, and it was thirty-five feet high. It's a pure wonder we didn't get drowned on one of those trips.

"Sometimes the crabs moved down into Virginia. When that happened, I wouldn't work too hard durin' the day. Wasn't any need to, wouldn't catch enough to make a difference anyway. Then, when dark came, I'd sail to Watts Island, about eight miles down into Virginia, and throw my scrapes over. I couldn't see to cull the crabs, so I'd feel each one in

Crab scraping under sail

the dark. If it was a soft crab, I'd put it in a bucket of water. All the rest I'd snap the claws and drop into baskets. Before dawn, I'd be back in Maryland. If they'd caught me, they'd have put me in jail and sold my boat, so I didn't dare let the sun come up on me down there, no matter how many crabs I was catchin'. I'd sail back to the creek, then I'd cull the crabs, sell 'em at a shanty, and go to bed.

"You wouldn't recognize the creek the way it was back then. Crab shanties lined the channel, at least twenty of 'em. A shanty had anywhere from six to twenty crabbers sellin' to it. Most of the shanty owners stayed there all day to tend to the crabs, but a couple of 'em crabbed themselves and hired old men for keepers. A big shanty required two keepers, they had that many crabs. Keepin' a shanty was right much work in those days. A keeper hauled the soft crabs to Crisfield in a sailboat, some even shoved around there in a skiff. Can you imagine somebody shovin' a skiff to Crisfield now, every day? They did back then. A man would shove a skiff an amazin' distance. I've known men who shoved a skiff all the way to Foxes Island, down in Virginia, just to catch a few crabs. Must be a fifteen mile round trip.

"A shanty keeper would net along the creek shore in the mornin' when he wasn't busy, catch a few crabs for extra money. Just before he went home that evenin', he'd drop a line over the edge of the wharf and catch a rockfish. Every shanty had rockfish around it, plenty of 'em. If he wanted to, a man could catch eight or ten five pounders in the evenin' without ever goin' out of the creek. We didn't though. We only caught as many as we were goin' to eat that day. We always had plenty to eat. Crabs and fish in the summer, fish and clams in the spring and fall, ducks and geese and oysters and man'ose in the winter. Oh, that was good eatin'. I can't think of anything I enjoy more than a stewed rockfish, one just caught fresh.

"Sometimes we hunted ducks, and sometimes we trapped 'em. Never seen a duck trap, have you? We made 'em from net, spread corn around, the ducks would follow the trail of corn into the trap. The door was hinged at the top, they'd push under it for the corn, then they couldn't get back out.

"I had some pet ducks back then. I found 'em in the marsh when they were just little balls of yellow fuzz with big black feet, fed 'em oats at first, then gave 'em cracked grain 'til they grew enough to look out for themselves. They lived in the marsh in back of the house, hung around the kitchen door lookin' for scraps. When I was goin' huntin', I'd get my gun and go out in the back yard and call 'em. They'd come waddlin' up out of the marsh. I'd throw my gun across my shoulder and start out walkin' to the creek, and those ducks would follow along behind, flappin' and runnin' on their tip toes to keep up. When I came to my skiff, they'd hop in. They'd ride on the foredeck or sit in the bottom while I shoved it out into the creek. When I reached my skipjack, they'd hop up on it. I'd raise my sail and start out for the huntin' marsh, with my skiff towin' along behind and my ducks sittin' on the deck. Once I reached the marsh, I'd anchor and lower the sail, pull the skiff up so the ducks could jump down into it, then I'd climb in and paddle into the marsh. I'd shove the skiff into some high sedges so I wouldn't be too conspicuous, then my ducks would jump out and swim around in the water beside me. If they started quackin', I knew somethin' was about to happen, so I'd get down low in the skiff. Pretty soon, a flock would come wingin' in. I'd stand up and fire into 'em, paddle out to pick up the ones I had killed, push the skiff back up into the sedges, and sit back to wait for some more.

"I wasn't the only waterman who had live decoys, but I

was the only one I knew of with pet ones. Most everybody else had ducks they had crippled with shot early in the season. They kept 'em in pens at home and tied weights to 'em when they carried 'em to the marsh so they couldn't get away. But I didn't have to worry about mine gettin' away, they enjoyed huntin' as much as I did.

"When I had enough huntin' for the day, I called my ducks and they climbed into the skiff. I paddled back to the skipjack and they flapped up onto it. I sailed back to the creek and they flopped down into the skiff for me to paddle 'em ashore. I walked home with the ducks I had killed in a burlap bag over one shoulder and my shotgun over the other, and my ducks waddled back into the marsh behind the house.

"That's the way it was in those days. The laws didn't mean a thing to us. We didn't mind huntin' with live decoys or crabbin' in Virginia, but we wouldn't think of workin' on a Sunday. The women cooked Sunday dinner on Saturday. Come Sunday mornin', we'd be at church by nine. We'd get out at noon if the preacher wasn't too long winded, then we'd eat dinner. We'd go back to church for Bible study at two and stay 'til five. We'd eat supper and then we'd go back to church. Youth meetin' was at seven, preachin' started at eight.

"I know I'm borin' you to death, Glenn. Why don't you turn on the television. Might be somethin' interestin' on it."

I assured Elmer I didn't care to watch television.

"Don't know why anybody would want to listen to me tell about what happened so long ago," he said as he put down the steering wheel he had been carving. "Time to start supper. Won't you stay and have some stew? It'll be ready in just a few minutes."

"No, thanks. I'm expected home for supper."

"You know you're welcome, Glenn. Somebody brought

me a nice terrapin. Mighty good if you know how to cook it. You ever had terrapin stew?"

"No, never did."

Elmer turned on the faucet, stuck a big potato under the running water, and scrubbed it with his bare hands.

"Summers we were plagued by mosquitoes," he said as he began peeling the potato. "We'd sit out under the trees 'til the house cooled off some, with a fire smolderin' to keep down the mosquitoes. When it came time to go to bed, somebody would take a bucket full of smolderin' grass inside the house to smoke out any mosquitoes. We'd hang burlap over the windows to try to keep 'em out, but it didn't. They'd nearly eat us alive on a calm night.

"Winters were worse, then we had to be concerned about ice. After Christmas, we rarely ventured very far from home to drudge for oysters, 'cause a freeze might catch us out and we couldn't get back to port. We had a bad freeze right after I got married, couldn't oyster for weeks, couldn't make a cent. Food was gettin' low, so me and a neighbor decided to go look for some man'ose. We knew the tide ran strong through Broad Creek and it was likely to be open. There were plenty of man'ose at the other end, where it comes out in the Pocomoke Sound, so we pulled a skiff across the ice from Jenkins Creek to Broad Creek, that's about a mile, and sure enough, the water was runnin' free. We launched the skiff, raised our sail, and took off for the Pocomoke with a strong nor'west wind behind us. We each had a spade for diggin' man'ose, and a gun in case we happened across some ducks. We were near the Pocomoke when we saw a flock of canvasbacks comin'. We got so excited about the ducks that we let the wind whip the sail across us and we capsized. Good thing for us the water was shallow, but the temperature was way below freezin' and the wind was blowin' awfully strong. We saved the spades and the guns, but we knew we would freeze to death before we could get back home.

"My neighbor had some matches in his shirt pocket and, thank the good Lord, they were dry. We lit some marsh grass and stood to the lee side of it to get warm, took our clothes off and held 'em up to the fire. They were already stiff with ice, and our skin had turned blue, never been so cold in my life. After we dried out, we climbed back in the boat and kept goin' for the Pocomoke. We dug about a bushel of man'ose and started back home, sailin' head wind. As we neared the north end of Broad Creek, I looked to the nor'west and saw a white cloud, only about five or six feet high, churnin' across the ice towards us. When it hit us I felt just like I had been shot. It was a gale of wind carryin' pellets of icy snow. We were only a little over a mile from home, so we abandoned the skiff and the man'ose right there and struck out across the ice. The next day, after the gale had let up, we dragged the skiff home. Good as those man'ose were, we never went back for more that winter."

While I was near the docks the next day I remembered how much Elmer liked fresh fish, so I stopped in the fish market to see what they had. I knew that fish had become scarce around Crisfield, but I was surprised to see only about a dozen spread on the crushed ice in the display case. I picked out a nice, plump flounder.

The market keeper plopped it on the scales to weigh it.

"Can't get one any fresher than this," he said. "Just came in on the truck from Ocean City this mornin'."

Chapter 7
A Time of Impoverishment

The afternoon was terribly hot. Once the wind died, swarms of mosquitoes and biting black flies rose from the fields around the house. This was the kind of a day when everyone stayed indoors with the air conditioner running full blast. That is, everyone stayed in except Hon, he would be at the shanty. When I was a boy, before anyone in our little community had heard of air conditioning, the waterman's shanty was his haven against the summer heat. It stood on its pilings out near the middle of the creek, just above the waters that were cooled by every change of the tide, its doors flung wide open to catch any breeze that might whiff in from the Bay.

The more I thought about it, the more the shanty seemed like a good place to be, away from the television and the chatter of Margaret and Virginia as they puttered around the house planning supper and thinking of things for me to do. I found Hon in the shade on the south wharf scrubbing crab pots with a stiff brush.

"I never used to have to do this," he said. "Just about the time the grass began to disappear from the bottom, this slimy moss started catchin' on my pots. Now I have to bring about twenty pots home every few days to clean 'em. The crabs won't go inside when they're covered with this mess."

Footsteps on the wharf warned us someone was coming.

"Not anybody I know," Hon said as he peered around the corner of the shanty. "Must be from the city, 'cause they didn't buy a car like that around here."

A short, skinny man rounded the corner with his chubby friend puffing along behind.

"Got any soft crabs?" the skinny man asked. We could tell immediately that he was from Baltimore.

"Pick of the crop," Hon replied as he put down his brush. "Come on in the shanty."

He swung the big, insulated door of the cooler open and pulled out a stack of trays.

"Close the door for me, Glenn," he said as he spread the trays across his workbench by the window and turned on the light over them.

"How much for these big ones?"

"Twelve dollars a dozen," Hon said.

"I'll give you ten."

"Thirteen," Hon countered.

"Thirteen! But you started at twelve!"

"I charge extra for bargainin'."

When they complained about that, Hon threatened to raise the price again, so they each put thirteen dollars on the bench. Hon counted out two dozen plump crabs, then threw in an extra for each of them, and stuffed their money in his right front pocket.

"I thought you were going to lose that sale," I said as they walked away down the wharf.

"Wouldn't bother me if I did," Hon replied. "I don't have a lot of patience dealing with a man who drives a new Mercedes and tries to chisel a dollar off my price, hard as I work."

The shanty was always more than just a place to keep crabs. It was a place of refuge where a man could go to get away from the commotion of the world and the responsibilities around the house. My grandfather made optimum use of his shanty this way. One time our kitchen chimney caught fire just as we were finishing supper. My grandmother shouted for him to get a bucket of water and put it out.

"Don't have time," he called back as he bolted out the front door. "Gotta go tend to the shanty."

My grandfather was named Lawrence, he was Bates Lawson's youngest son. He married Bessie, the only child of Thomas and Suzie Byrd. Floyd and Margaret lived with them when I was born, and when Hon was born, and when our brother Larry was born. Money was tight, but not nearly as tight as we were in the two bedroom house Thomas had built fifty years before.

So Floyd and Margaret had to find another place to live, whether they could afford it or not. A neighbor a few hundred yards closer to the creek moved to the city to find work. They bought his house and hauled what little furniture they owned to it. Hon and Larry went along, but I stayed with Bessie because she needed someone to haul coal and water and kerosene when Lawrence was on his boat or at the shanty, which was most of the time.

To cope with the dwindling seafood supply and meet his house payments, Floyd had to leave the water for awhile. He took a job driving a truck. Lawrence's approach was different. He rarely bought anything.

I never understood how Lawrence earned his meager living until he took me crabbing one summer morning. He woke me well before dawn, the earliest I had ever climbed out of bed in my entire six years. After a breakfast of cold biscuits and molasses by the flickering light of our kerosene lamp, I followed him out the door and along the dark road toward the creek. When we reached the marsh, he turned onto a path that led through the bushes to the creek bank where he kept his flat-bottomed skiff. With a few quick strokes of a wooden scoop that he had carved himself, he dashed out the water that had accumulated overnight. He lifted me aboard, untied the frayed mooring line, and began to pole us along in the shallow water. I still remember being surprised at how swiftly he could pole the skiff, even though we were headed into a stiff breeze.

We splashed our way through the watery darkness for about a hundred yards with the salt spray whipping up over the tiny foredeck and spattering on my face. We came astern his other boat, swinging from a pole sticking up in the shallow water. This old boat was about sixteen feet long, not much bigger than the skiff, but it was built much heavier and it had a one cylinder motor just a little aft of its center seat. Lawrence held the skiff against the boat while I climbed in, then he stepped in himself. He tied the skiff to a cleat on the stern, and then he cast us adrift from the pole.

He spun the fly wheel by hand to start the old motor. Shortly after we cleared the other boats that were moored nearby, we came to a cluster of shanties standing high on pilings near the mouth of the creek. A glow showed at the windows of a couple of them. Lawrence aimed for a dark one, cut his motor off, and coasted up alongside the wharf. He tied the boat to a piling, lifted me up onto the wharf, and led me inside. I curled up in a pile of dry eel grass and quickly fell asleep as he took his lantern out on the back wharf to look at the crabs in his pound.

When he woke me and put me back into his boat, the eastern sky was just beginning to turn gray. He spun the flywheel and we were off again, this time headed out of the creek into the wide waters of the river. The wind was still blowing, the spray was flying, and the waves were frighteningly high, at least to me. I turned around and shouted to him that I was scared because I couldn't swim.

"Don't worry, I can't swim neither," he shouted back.

We were soon across the open water, sheltered from the wind and waves by the Cedar Island shoreline. Lawrence continued westward, keeping about a hundred yards offshore until we came to a narrow creek that led into the marsh. He turned into the creek and slowed the motor. We rounded a bend and a huge pond opened up before us. He cut the motor off, picked up a heavy block of scrap iron, and tossed it overboard for an anchor.

He untied the skiff and pulled it up beside the boat so I could climb into it. He slid a long handled dip net out from under the seat, stepped up on the tiny foredeck, and began to paddle with his net as he stared down through the shallow water at the grassy bottom ahead of him.

He had only paddled a couple of easy strokes when he jabbed his net down, swerving the skiff sharply to the left. He stabbed into the water ahead of him and scooped up his first crab of the day. He reached into the net with his bare hand, stretched a fin out, and glanced at it in the early morning light. He declared, "It's a good'un", snapped both claws so it wouldn't be able to pinch him, and gently dropped the crab into a bushel basket in the bottom of the skiff.

I decided to try to help him, so I peered over the side to see if I could spot a crab. Just below the surface of the water, a thick mat of long, stringy eel grass stretched out in every direction, interrupted by an occasional small patch of bare mud. All kinds of little, swimming creatures, fish and eels and others I didn't recognize, were magnified by the crystal clear water.

Then I saw a movement in the grass. I pointed to it and shouted excitedly, "A crab! There's a crab!"

He didn't even turn his head.

"I saw it, tain't no good," he muttered and kept paddling, staring into the water ahead.

I decided that I had a lot to learn before I could be of any help, so I settled back on my plank seat for lesson number one on how to become a waterman, just watching someone who knew what he was doing. This was the way the training had been passed along from generation to generation.

He kept only the peeler crabs, the ones that would shed their hard shells within three or four days. The rest he tossed overboard. He could usually tell if a crab was a peeler or not as soon as he caught it, but occasionally he held one up to the bright sky and squinted for a closer look at the sign. If he caught a double crab, which was a big, angry male grasping another crab that he knew was a female peeler ready to shed, he flipped them into the air with his net. The male let go as they fell. Lawrence caught the peeler with his net, allowing the troublesome male to drop into the water.

When he was fortunate enough to catch a soft crab or a buster, which was a crab that had already popped its hard shell open along the back rim and was beginning to work its way loose, he gently dropped it into a bucket of water. Any crabs that were not keepers, he returned to the water unharmed. Eventually, they would also become peelers.

As we slowly worked our way around the big pond, we came to a place where the wind was whipping across an unsheltered stretch of water, covering it with ripples so I couldn't see the bottom. Lawrence reached under the foredeck and pulled out a flask about the size of a cough medicine bottle. It had a cork stopper with a small hole in it, and when

Crab netter

he flung a stream of droplets from it, the ripples disappeared like magic so we could see the bottom again. I asked what he had spread on the water.

"Fish oil," he replied. He stuck the flask in his pocket and went back to his netting. Every time the ripples bothered him, he flung out a stream, smoothing the water for another five or ten minutes.

The gentle breeze kept us from becoming too hot, but the crabs in the basket began to stir around. Lawrence nosed the skiff against the marshy shore, picked up a double handful of dried eel grass, dipped it in the water, then scattered it over the crabs in the basket. I swatted frantically at the mosquitoes while he went ashore again, snapped leafy branches from some bushes, and spread them on top of the grass. When he shoved the skiff away from the shore, into the wind, the swarming mosquitoes disappeared. I hoped he wouldn't need to go ashore again.

He returned to his methodical search of the pond. Crabs were his primary prey, but he occasionally scooped up an oyster which he dropped onto the floor of the skiff.

A flounder rose from the mud and scooted off, narrowly escaping his net. "That would've tasted good for supper," he said, but he made no attempt to chase after it. He had but one chance at anything that could swim. Only the oysters were easy to catch, everything else he had to get with his first jab, and he did so almost every time.

As the sun climbed higher, the air became perfectly still and shimmering waves of heat rose from the marsh. Lawrence shoved out toward the middle of the pond, stuck the handle of his crab net into the muddy bottom, and tied the skiff to it so we would not drift close to shore. He pulled his pail from under the seat and handed me the jar of water and a dry biscuit.

"Goin' to be a thunderstorm this afternoon. We better not tarry too much longer," he said.

I looked up, but I didn't see any storm clouds.

"How can you tell?" I asked.

"I just know."

After he had eaten his biscuit and taken a sip from the jar, he worked his way back to his other boat. I scrambled aboard as he held the skiff up against it. As soon as I was safely seated, he set his basket of peelers in front of me and his bucket of soft crabs behind me. He pulled up the chunk of iron and slid it under the foredeck, then spun the flywheel to start the motor. With the skiff towing along behind, we snaked our way out of the creek and headed across the open water of the river toward home. I looked back, but I couldn't make out the opening we had just left. It seemed to have disappeared into the marshy shoreline, and the narrow boat left no wake to show me where we had been.

We rounded the bar that sheltered the mouth of Jenkins Creek and we passed through shanty town. Lawrence cut off the motor, coasted in a sweeping, half circle to his shanty, bumped up against the wharf, grabbed a piling, and tied a line to it. He set the bucket onto the wharf first, then the basket. The tide was much higher than it had been in the morning, so I climbed out of the boat without any help.

I followed him through the shanty to the back wharf. Here was his pound, protected from the beating waves by a fence of rough boards nailed to poles that stuck up out of the muddy bottom. He told me that he had found the boards along the shore. They must have washed off the deck of an old bugeye hauling lumber up the Bay in a storm. He had cut the locust poles from the woods behind our house.

Two rows of shedding floats, like half submerged chicken

coops, were staked out in the pound and three other floats were tied to the wharf. He sat down on a low, weathered bench and began to sort through his basket of crabs. He squinted at the sign on each and then tossed it into one of the floats tied to the wharf.

When he had finished sorting the day's catch, he stepped down from the wharf into a tiny skiff and paddled over to one of the other floats in the pound. He stirred around in it with a short handled net to get the crabs moving, scooped out the empty crab shells, and tossed them overboard. Then he began dipping up soft crabs, gently dropping each into his bucket of water. He found a dead crab, broke it in half, and tossed it overboard near the wharf.

When he was satisfied that he had dipped all the soft crabs from this float, he moved on to the next. After checking all the floats in the pound, he paddled back to the wharf and carried the bucket inside. I followed along to watch. I was eager to learn how to become a crabber and tend a shanty so I could quit school and make a lot of money like the older boys on the creek.

He set the bucket on a waist high bench beside a wooden tray. The tray was divided by a slat down the middle, on each side were rows of crabs neatly packed in a thin layer of grass. He took the crabs from his bucket and gently added them to the rows, then grabbed a handful of dry eel grass from under the bench and scattered a layer of it over them. He reached down into a nearby box full of eel grass and lifted out a block of ice, shaved off a snowball size pile of flakes with a big scraper, and spread them on the tray.

"Guess I'd better launch a float," he muttered. He pulled his tiny skiff up to the back wharf, stepped down into it, and paddled across the pound to a rack where a couple of floats were pulled up to dry. He dragged one of them off, and towed it over to a float that had become waterlogged and sunken lower than the others. With his dip net, he bailed the crabs out of this float and into the one he had just launched. Then he towed the half sunken float back to the rack and struggled to pull it up. He scrubbed a hairy layer of green scum from the float with a long handled brush, splashed a couple of buckets of water into it, and paddled back to the wharf.

Just inside the shanty door was a ball of twine with a hook dangling from it. He took a dead soft crab, broke it into quarters, and slipped one piece onto the hook. Then he dropped it over the edge of the wharf, about where he had tossed the other dead crab when he was fishing out his floats. He held the line still for a few seconds. When it wiggled, he jerked it upward and dragged a thrashing rockfish to the surface. He dropped the squirming fish into a basket, put a handful of dead crabs and a pinch of ice in his pail, and set both in his boat along with two trays covered by a wet sack.

He motored back to his stake, tied to it, transferred the trays and the bucket and the basket to his skiff, tossed the oysters he had caught into the water near the stake, and paddled to the landing. Here, he pulled his skiff up onto the sandy beach beside the road, walked over to the store, ordered two Cokes for us, and sat down in the shade of the porch to talk with the other crabbers.

After a while, a pickup truck with rasping brakes stopped beside the landing. Lawrence and a couple of the other crabbers got up and walked across the road to their skiffs, carried their trays to the pickup, and set them on the tailgate. The driver rolled back the layer of eel grass covering each tray, counted the crabs, and wrote down the number on a tally sheet.

I climbed into the skiff and he shoved back to the marsh

bank where we had started that morning. He jammed his paddle down into the mud and tied his skiff to it. He picked the stiff rockfish out of the basket and plopped it head first into his pail with the dead crabs. I proudly followed behind him as he pushed his way through the bushes toward the oyster shell road. I had just completed the first day of what I dreamed would be a long career.

Bessie fried the soft crabs for us as soon as we got home. I ate my fill, fed the leftovers to our cat, climbed the stairs, and dropped into bed. I awoke to the boom of thunder. Sheets of rain beat against the window and a violent wind shook the house. I hurried downstairs where I found Bessie in her rocking chair, sewing. Lawrence was gone. I knew he would be, he had to go tend to the shanty.

When I think back to my grandfather, I can see that his way of life had changed little from that of his ancestors, even as far back as colonial times. He was a hunter and a gatherer. For meat, we ate mostly the fish and crabs and ducks and oysters and mananose that he brought home in his pail. My grandmother kept a vegetable garden and fruit trees, but he preferred the wild asparagus and winter cress and blackberries that he picked along the edge of the marsh. He never saw the need to buy nor plant so long as he could just go out and find something to put on the table.

He had a motor in his boat, but he could have gotten along just about as well with a sail. He had no running water, no power equipment, no electricity, and no radio. For tools he had a hammer and a hand saw and pulleys and wedges and levers. He let the water do much of his lifting. When he needed to paint the bottom of his old boat, he just floated it onto a couple of sunken logs at high tide. When the waters receded it would be sitting up dry. He had six hours to paint it before the incoming tide reached it again.

He watched the seagulls, the wind, and the sky to determine what kind of weather was coming. He kept his schedule by the sun and by the rising and falling of the tides. He didn't own a car. When he traveled by land, he avoided the roads and walked the paths through the woods and marshes. Most of his travel, though, was by boat along the waters of the Bay and the sounds and rivers and creeks, the old colonial highway.

Lawrence was content with his station in life. He enjoyed his work, his family, his friends, and his freedom. He saw no need to change.

Chapter 8
A Time of Adjusting

Larry, my youngest brother, called from his home in Texas to remind me that Floyd and Margaret would soon be celebrating their fiftieth wedding anniversary. He and Hon and I had talked several times about giving them a nice party, but since the three of us lived so many miles apart we had not made much headway with the plans. We decided we should let Hon take care of all the arrangements, since he lived right across the road from them and would know what customarily was being done in town for occasions such as that. Larry and I told him that he could do whatever he thought was best and we would each pay a third of the expenses. That seemed safe enough to us, for we knew that times were hard on the water and he was struggling just to make ends meet. Hon chartered a double deck cruise ship and printed a hundred fifty invitations.

"Can we afford it, Hon?" I asked. "After all, you haven't paid the bank what you borrowed to start crabbing this spring."

"They'll only have a fiftieth anniversary once," he answered. "I'll be broke lots more times."

The cruise didn't cost as much as I had feared. Hon worked out a good price with the skipper because we would be using the ship at a time when it ordinarily was moored and not making any money at all. We left the Crisfield docks about a half hour before sunset, cruised out of the river and then southward on the Tangier Sound while Floyd and Margaret accepted congratulations from their friends and opened their gifts. As we neared Tangier Island, the skipper swung the ship in a wide turn and headed back to Crisfield with the moon shining brightly overhead and the navigational beacons flashing all around us. Larry and I agreed that Hon had planned a fitting party for a man who spent most of his life on those waters.

Floyd was a true waterman. He had been a haul seiner, a gill netter, a crabber, a tonger, and he had also been an outlaw hunter and an oyster pirate.

Back when we still lived with my grandparents, I remember Margaret playfully chasing Hon and me upstairs to the cold bedroom and tucking us in, then going back down to plead with Floyd not to go out in the boat that night. We quietly listened while she argued that they did not need the money badly enough for him to be an outlaw, but he went anyway. If we stayed awake a little while longer, we could hear the distant rumble of the big boat's motor, and we would know that he was starting out for his night's work on the dark waters of the Pocomoke Sound.

During the winter he teamed up with another waterman I will call Pard. That was not his name, but I will call him that just in case his descendants might be embarrassed by me telling of his illegal activities. Floyd had been very careful in choosing Pard. He wanted someone he could trust his life with, for that is just what their kind of work amounted to.

Floyd didn't have a car, so he walked to the creek Sunday night after dark to meet Pard. Each of them climbed into his own skiff and paddled out to the big boat swinging from a stake in the deep water. Towing their skiffs behind the boat, they slowly motored out of the dark, twisting creek and then, with only a compass, a pocket watch, and a gauge showing the revolutions of the motor, they turned off every light on the boat and ran straight out to where they would work that night, usually an oyster rock across the line in Virginia. When they reached the vicinity of the rock, Pard slowed the boat while Floyd picked up a long sounding pole and began stabbing into the water alongside the boat, probing the bottom. As soon as he struck something hard he knew he was over the oyster rock, so he tossed overboard a jar containing a flashlight to mark the spot while Pard threw a drudge over the stern. When they felt they had dragged it far enough, they stopped the boat and hauled the heavy, oyster clogged drudge in by hand, then turned the boat around and dragged past the floating flashlight again.

An hour of this back breaking work and they would have the boat loaded with oysters. Then they headed for a familiar cove in Maryland to anchor for the night. The next morning they got up before the sun, ran to Crisfield to sell their catch, and went back out to spend the rest of the day tonging legally.

Hand tonging was hard work. Floyd stood on the edge of the deck with the toes of his boots against a rail that was only about an inch and a half high. That was all that kept him from slipping off the boat as it swung at its anchor line and bobbed in the waves. He probed along the bottom with his tongs, in water as much as fifteen feet deep, until he felt a clump of oysters. Then he forced the shafts together, clenching in the teeth of the rakes any oysters and shells and anything else that happened to be down there. He hauled the long shafts up, hand over hand, and dumped the oysters onto the culling board for Pard to sort through. He continued plunging his tongs into the water, forcing the shafts together, hauling them up, and dumping them until his arms felt heavy as lead. Then, for a break, he changed places with Pard and picked up the culling hammer, knocked the shells and smaller oysters loose from the legal sized ones, tossed the good oysters onto a pile in the bottom of the boat, and brushed the small ones and the shells and the trash overboard.

They stopped work soon enough in the afternoon to run to a harbor in the daylight. They liked to anchor in a cove on the south side of Cedar Island, within sight of the Foxes Island hunting club house. This club house was just a short distance over the boundary line, on a marshy island in Virginia. Most of the members were wealthy Virginians who were influential enough to keep the game wardens away, but that didn't help them. They couldn't shoot well enough to kill their limit, anyway. They wanted to carry photos home that they would be proud of, so when they saw Floyd and Pard anchor nearby, they sent their guide across the line to the boat. The guide offered to purchase as many geese as Floyd and Pard could kill.

The geese normally stayed out in the open water during the day, but at night they flew in at low tide and pitched near the shore to feed. Floyd set the alarm clock to go off about the time he figured the geese would be coming in, then he and Pard climbed into their bunks to catch a few winks. When the alarm jarred them awake they dressed warmly, stepped out of the dark cabin into the hold where the day's oysters were stored, grabbed their shovels, and cleared the oysters away from the removable boards that concealed their big guns.

Pard's gun was about seven feet long with a barrel that measured two inches across the bore. Pard called it a skiffing gun, because he had to mount it on a skiff before he could fire it. Floyd's gun was about two or three feet longer than Pard's, and its bore was big enough that Pard's barrel would fit inside. They called Floyd's gun a cannon. They didn't even have to fire these guns to be breaking the law. Just owning one of them had been illegal for many years.

They loaded the two guns before they put them in the skiffs. They measured their black powder with a horn that looked very much like one I had seen Daniel Boone holding in a picture. After they packed the powder down, they rammed a pound of shot into the muzzle. They mounted a gun on each skiff and tossed a sack of eel grass in behind it. Then they primed the guns and shoved off in search of the geese they knew were feeding somewhere nearby.

Floyd and Pard each stood in his skiff and poled it with a long paddle through the shallow water, looking for the geese. If the moon was shining they could see them, but if the sky was overcast they had to listen for the faint splashing and the bubbles of the geese feeding on grass in the shallow water. When they found a flock, they quietly slipped the long paddles into the floors of their skiffs and took out their short paddles. With one of these in each hand, they kneeled down in their boats and sneaked up on the feeding geese, being careful all the while not to jar their own gun and accidentally fire it, or get in front of the other gun's muzzle. They kept their skiffs close together and when they lined up with a cluster of geese, they fired.

The big guns blasted in unison and slammed back against the sacks of grass, driving the two skiffs stern first through the water. A black cloud shot out across the water, obscuring the frenzied geese that were now beating their way into the air and scattering in every direction. Back home, several miles away, in a house closed up against the cold with a stove burning in the living room, we could hear the muffled roar of the big guns if the wind wasn't blowing.

Floyd and Pard picked the dead geese from the water and paddled back as quickly as they could, for it was now no secret that they were hunting with the big guns. And, of course, they each killed over the legal limit every time they shot. If they couldn't get enough geese in front of them so they would kill fifteen or more, they didn't fire. Pard's gun could easily kill fifteen with a single shot, Floyd's could kill over thirty. They hid the guns and the geese, sometimes under the floor boards of the boat and other times under the ridge of dried eel grass that rimmed the shore line of the marsh, and then they climbed back into their bunks to finish the night's sleep. Early the next morning they sold their geese to the guide from the hunting club and headed back out to the oyster rock.

This is the way they spent the winter, tonging for oysters during the daylight hours and alternating between drudging and hunting with their big guns at night. If they couldn't sell their geese to sportsmen at the club, they carried them to town with their oysters and sold them to a fish market. The owner sent a hired man with a wheelbarrow down to the dock. Sometimes they brought in so many that the man would need to make two or three trips with the wheelbarrow, hauling burlap bags full of illegal geese half way across town. A lot of people knew what was in the bags, but nobody reported them. Even though this was in the 1940s, Crisfield was still a lawless town whenever conservation regulations were concerned.

Pard had bought his gun at the Crisfield water department. Floyd told me a plumber made them in his spare time from the town's inventory of pipe. He used a two inch water pipe for the barrel, then he strengthened the firing chamber by forcing a larger pipe over that end of the barrel and welding the two together. He made the trigger and hammer himself, and he carved the stock. His guns were not very pretty, but they were cheap and deadly efficient. He didn't charge Pard money for the gun, he asked to be paid in ducks and geese.

145

Floyd's gun was manufactured in England. The barrel was uniformly tapered from the thick walled firing chamber to the thinner wall at the muzzle end. The trigger and hammer assembly were machine made, and the stock was carved by a local decoy maker. Floyd's gun was first class. It looked much like a normal rifle, except it was considerably bigger. During the off season, he stored it in the stairway to our upstairs bedrooms. It was too long for him to stand it up anywhere else in the house.

Floyd and Pard were involved in a very dangerous trade. Besides the normal hazards of falling into the cold water or being caught by a sudden winter storm, they were working at night without lights and they were firing big guns. The chance of drowning was great enough when they could see what they were doing, it increased dramatically in the dark. And whenever they fired the big guns, they never knew what would happen. One night, the recoil of Pard's gun threw him overboard and dazed him. Fortunately, the water was shallow and Floyd was there to help him back into his skiff. Another time, the firing chamber of Pard's gun exploded, spraying shrapnel across the water on the opposite side of the boat from him. There was also the chance that when the big gun fired it would scoot over the sack of grass, slam into the stern of the skiff, and knock it out. This happened to another waterman from Jenkins Creek, leaving him standing waist deep in the cold water, miles from the Maryland shore with a huge, illegal gun in his hands and a sunken skiff beneath his feet.

If Floyd and Pard had been caught they would have been put in prison and all of their equipment, the guns, the skiffs, and even the big boat would have been confiscated. But they were never caught. Their boat was fast, and they only spent a short time out on the oyster rocks with their drudges in the water. If they had seen a police boat coming they would have just cut the drudge line with a hatchet and run for the shallows. The police boat was deeper draft than theirs and could not follow them. The drudge line had a buoy and a sack of salt tied to it. The sack of salt was to make it sink so the police would not find it. The buoy was to float it when the salt dissolved, so Floyd and Pard could go back later and pick it up.

They didn't worry about a game warden catching them at night, because the wardens worked alone and the market hunters worked in pairs. No one man in his right mind would attempt to arrest two armed, illegal hunters in the dark, isolated marshes of that no man's land along the boundary line between the two states.

For all of this hard, hazardous, illegal work, you would think Floyd made good money. Not so. Oysters were becoming scarce, but still they were not priced very high. The extra income was the reason Floyd gave for his moonlighting, but years later he told me that he did it mostly because he enjoyed it.

Floyd and Margaret learned to get by cheaply. Floyd had a boat because he needed one for his work, but he didn't have a car or even a pickup truck. He didn't drink or smoke or gamble, and the only times I can think of us spending money frivolously was on Saturday nights. We dressed in our best and walked the two miles to Crisfield, where Hon and I wandered through the stores on Main Street with Margaret while she picked up sewing thread or whatever she needed around the house and Floyd visited with his friends on the crowded sidewalk. Hon and I then followed them to the ticket booth of the New Arcade Theatre, where Floyd paid seventy cents admission to get the four of us in to see the motion picture show. Larry was still a baby, so our grandmother took care of him during those nights on the town.

We didn't spend a lot of money on clothes, either. Hon and I each had one good suit for church. In a day before they were fashionable, we wore jeans to school. They were reasonably priced and tough enough so we didn't tear them when we took the short cut home through the bushes along the edge of the marsh. The other kids wore flannel pants and carried peanut butter sandwiches for lunch, Hon and I wore jeans and carried wild duck.

Floyd, like most other watermen in our community, believed the government had overstepped its authority when it enacted legislation that limited the number of ducks and geese a man could kill and the number of oysters he could catch. He firmly held to his conviction that God had given him the right to kill and sell waterfowl to support his family, and to catch all the oysters he could.

The conservation regulations on the Bay at that time fell into four categories. They were economic restrictions, limits, restriction of equipment, and licensing. Each category had a different purpose but the goal was the same, to prevent people from depleting some species of Bay life by hunting or fishing.

An economic restriction was designed to reduce the amount of money a person can make by hunting or fishing for a particular species. For example, watermen could no longer sell terrapin, so they stopped hunting them and spent their time catching crabs, which they could sell. Another regulation prohibited the sale of wildfowl, so hunters no longer openly slaughtered them by the hundreds. Since men enjoyed hunting them for food and for sport, this type of restriction didn't stop the killing of ducks and geese. It didn't even limit the killing enough to prevent the rapid decline of the duck population.

A limit was designed to control the population decline of

a species. For example, regulations limited the number of ducks a hunter could kill in one day, and the days in a year as well as the hours of a day when hunting was permitted. If the population of a certain type of duck continued to decline, the season for that duck could be reduced further, or the number a hunter could kill in a day could be reduced, or hunters could be limited from killing any at all.

A restriction of equipment reduced the amount a single hunter could take by reducing his efficiency. Oyster drudgers with power boats could go around and around until they wiped out an entire oyster bar, but a sailboat was not as maneuverable and not as destructive, so drudging was restricted to sailboats. Restrictions on duck hunters prohibited them from using automatic shotguns, using guns that fired large loads of shot, baiting ducks with corn, trapping ducks, or luring ducks with live decoys.

Licensing theoretically limited the number of people who were hunting or fishing, but not by much, because a license cost only a few dollars. To restrict the number of hunters and fishermen by raising the price of a license was not practical, for that would have made hunting the privilege of only the wealthy sportsmen. The impoverished watermen, who sometimes needed the ducks to feed their families, would have then turned the marshes into a war zone, and no man would have been safe there. The main effect of licensing was that it provided incentive to obey the other laws, for the license of a habitual offender could be revoked.

During the summers, Floyd turned perfectly legal. He was a crab scraper. He dragged two scrapes at a time behind his boat. As soon as he pulled one aboard by hand, he dumped it into his culling box and tossed it back into the water. He then bent to sorting out the peeler crabs from all the sea life that he had collected along with them. When he finished culling, he hauled the other scrape aboard, dumped it, tossed it back into the water, and started culling again. The crab scrape was an efficient piece of equipment, but with it Floyd became less of a hunter than Lawrence had been and more of a harvester. He still had the same freedom of movement a hunter enjoyed. He didn't have to make up his mind where he was going to work on any day until he crossed over the bar at the mouth of the creek and picked a direction to point the boat, but he didn't experience the exhilaration of a hunter. Instead, he merely seemed to be operating a crab catching machine.

The challenge was still there, though. He had to pick the right place, one that was free of submerged stumps. He had to drag the scrapes at the proper speed, he had to avoid the shallow bars where the boat would go aground, and he had to keep on the eel grass where the crabs would be hiding.

Floyd's scraping boat was a skipjack, twenty-four feet long with a very flat bottom so it could work in shallow water. It was so maneuverable it would practically turn around in its own length. It had low sides so he could pull the scrapes aboard without too much effort. It was a wonderful boat for crabbing, but it was not suited at all for oystering in the deeper waters during the harsh winters. He used a much bigger boat for that.

The first few years, Floyd sold his crabs to a shanty owner on Jenkins Creek. For some reason, he never shared Lawrence's shanty. Instead, when he felt he needed his own, he and a friend rented the shanty beside the vacant villa at Hammock Point, where the terrapin industry on the Bay had begun and near where his great, great grandfather had lived.

The location was not convenient. He had to paddle out to his boat and motor around to the point three times a day to tend to his live crabs. To him that was a nuisance, but I thought it was great because I tagged along for the ride. While he was working in the crab pound, I explored the cavernous rooms of the vacant house or waded along the shore or just sat and watched the boats going to and from the Crisfield harbor.

Then Floyd heard of a new invention, the crab pot. This was a cube shaped trap made of galvanized wire with a rope and a buoy attached. He bought a few of them and set them out in a row in the shallow waters along the edge of the Pocomoke Sound. He caught so many crabs with them that he bought another hundred and put his scrapes away.

He moved the pots further away from the shore, into water that was deep enough for his big boat, and he sold his scraping boat to eliminate that expense. With all the crabs he was catching, he was making more money than ever before, but he paid a price for it. He had to borrow from the bank for his new equipment, and he lost his freedom of movement. Every day, he knew exactly where he was going when he left the creek. He motored right out to his string of pots and began pulling them in and dumping them, just like an assembly line. No longer did he bear any resemblance to a hunter and a gatherer. He had become a small businessman with a fixed location, a significant investment, and weekly expenses to meet. He could no longer live only for today. He now had to think about bills and bank notes coming due tomorrow.

Another change took place, and I may have been the only person who noticed it. Floyd brought home two live Canada geese that he found in the marsh. I asked why he hadn't shot them, and he replied that the hunting season had ended. This is the first time I ever heard him admit that he was obligated to obey any conservation law.

The geese should have migrated back to Canada, but one of them had been shot and its wing was injured. The other goose was perfectly healthy, but geese mate for life and this one wouldn't abandon its crippled partner. Floyd brought them home because he knew that some other waterman would find them and illegally kill them. He hoped that in the safety of a big cage in our back yard the injured goose would heal sufficiently to fly again, and he could release them the following winter.

I was assigned the responsibility of making sure the geese were fed daily and always had plenty of water in their tub. I gave them corn and table scraps, and I poked fresh grass through the wire for them. In time, I gained their confidence enough so they would eat from my hand. I sat under the shade tree beside their pen and tried to imitate their grunts and their honks. I learned their warning cries and their calls to other geese that were flying overhead.

One day I carelessly left the door of the pen unlatched and the geese escaped. When I went to feed them, they were gone. I knew they were in the marsh behind the house, so I asked Hon to go with me to catch them. As we reached the edge of the marsh, I realized the futility of searching that many thousands of acres, and my heart sank. I knew they were nearly helpless, and would soon fall prey to a fox or a weasel or a hunter.

I called out with the honk I had learned from them, and they answered. Hon and I plunged into the marsh, honking and wading through the water that was sometimes up to our waists, until we found them. We chased them ashore into some bushes and caught them. Just before dark, we shoved the struggling geese back into their cage.

The most modern shanty on the creek belonged to Skinny, a man so thin that the end of his belt hung half way down to his knees. This shanty had electricity, and a cooler, and even a freezer. It even had a wharf that led across the marsh to the road. The pound was huge, more than enough for all the crabs Skinny could catch, so he bought crabs from other watermen and hired somebody to help him tend to them.

Normally, Skinny was the first man to leave the creek every morning. That way, he could work as long as anyone else and still get back to his shanty in time to buy crabs. He even slept in his boat some nights so he could get an early start. One morning as Floyd shoved his skiff out in the dim light just before the dawn, he noticed that Skinny's boat was still in the creek. Floyd thought it strange for Skinny to still be there, so he paddled over to check the boat and found Skinny crumpled on the floor behind the engine. His dangling belt had become entangled with a turning shaft. Floyd cut Skinny loose and took him to the hospital. He never regained consciousness.

Skinny's widow sold the shanty to Floyd. She told him that she believed Skinny would want him to have it, so she didn't offer anyone else a chance to buy it.

During the summers, Hon and I practically lived at that shanty. Hon spent more time there than I did, since he crewed with Floyd on the boat. I picked up odd jobs around town to earn spending money, but every day as soon as I finished work I headed for the shanty. Hon and I loved to listen to the old timers sit on the bench in the shade and tell their tales of what a waterman's life was like in their youth. We also swam in the creek, and we paddled Floyd's skiff out to the river every couple of weeks for a load of dried eel grass. It was piled up in waist deep rows along the shore. Floyd kept a big pile of the grass in the shanty all the time. He packed the crabs in it so they would not be bruised by their trip to the city markets, and he kept his block of ice in a box full of it. Margaret also had a use for the grass. She put it in a field beside the house until the rain washed the salt from it, then she spread it around the plants in her garden. It kept down the weeds and held the moisture in the ground during dry weather, and it added nutrients to the soil when it decomposed.

Floyd worked hard during the summer, and he made a decent living from his crab pots and his soft crab shedding business. During the winter he worked just as hard, but oysters were becoming scarcer all the time. He could see hope for the future, though, for research by the states of Maryland and Virginia was shedding more light on the oyster's life cycle, and both states began to take steps to revive the industry.

When the waters of the Chesapeake warm sufficiently under the summer sun, the oysters spawn clouds of tiny yellow eggs. An oyster of average size can release more than seventy million eggs in a single spawn, and can repeat the spawns at three to seven day intervals until it has released as many as five hundred million eggs in a single season. Fertilized eggs, called larva, are about the size of a needle point. They swim freely for two to three weeks, and some for as long as nine weeks, seeking a firm place to attach. They fasten themselves to pilings, or to lost anchors, or even inside sunken bottles, but they favor oyster shells. They tend to grow in clusters, either on empty shells or on living oysters. A cluster attracts additional larva and continues to expand in size until, after hundreds of years of growth, it can become an oyster bar covering acres of bottom.

A larva that has attached itself to something firm is called a spat. Within one month after a spat has set, it has grown to the diameter of a pea. Within a year, it is a miniature oyster the size of a quarter. Growth continues at the rate of about an inch a year, with some reaching a length of twelve inches or more.

In areas most favorable to spawning, spat can set thickly enough that the oysters are too crowded to allow growth. Long ago, watermen recognized the best areas for spat to set. Even in colonial times, they moved small oysters from these beds and spread them in creeks near their homes. They called the small oysters 'seed', and referred to this practice as 'planting'.

The states of Maryland and Virginia both realized that to restore the oysters, some action other than merely restricting the waterman was necessary, so both governments became involved in oyster propagation, and set aside the best spat catching areas as reserves for growing seed. Virginia tended to encourage individuals to lease bottom from the state and buy seed oysters to plant. Maryland watermen strongly resisted the leasing of bottom, so that state's Tidewater Fisheries Division of the Department of Natural Resources was assigned the responsibility for managing the oyster planting on public bottom. This planting program was to be paid for by a tax on oysters unloaded at the dock.

Maryland also enacted legislation that required oyster shells to be collected and returned to the Bay bottom in the spring to serve as clutch for the new spawn. This responsibility was assigned to the Tidewater Fisheries as well, and was also financed by the tax on oysters.

With the state recognizing that it needed to play a leading role in the restoration of the Chesapeake seafood industry, prospects for the future brightened. Even so, being a waterman promised to remain a tough and a risky way to make a living. Nobody was more aware of that than the watermen and their wives. After I went to bed one night, I heard talking

155

downstairs. Margaret and Floyd and my grandparents were discussing my future. To them, the best job in town belonged to the bookkeeper at the seafood broker's house. He worked indoors, out of the summer heat and the winter winds, and he could depend on a paycheck every week. Maybe I could get a job as good as that bookkeeper if I went to college. Maybe I should be the first one in our family to leave the water.

I heard Margaret and Floyd say they would try to pay half of my tuition. My grandparents offered to set aside five dollars a week from their social security for my spending money, and I would have to save what I made during the summer to cover the remainder.

I attended a state supported college for a couple of years. Then summer work became scarce, and I was not able to put much in the bank. I knew I could earn education money by serving in the military, so I walked to Crisfield and asked the lady at the draft board to put my name at the top of the list. She said she'd be happy to do it. Most of the boys in town wouldn't mind if I went ahead of them.

My induction notice came the next month. As sunset neared on the day before I was to board the bus, I walked to the shanty and untied one of the little boats. I yanked the outboard's starter cord and pointed the bow toward the Bay. The red glow in the west had disappeared and the creek banks were only shadows when I returned to the shanty wharf. I threw the line around one of the pilings and looked back at the water shimmering in the moonlight.

I wondered if I would ever come back to Jenkins Creek again.

Chapter 9
A Time of Despairing

"Hon was in court last week," Margaret said.

"What was he charged with?" I asked.

"Nothing, but he almost got locked up anyway. Don't ask me to explain it. You'll have to talk to him if you want to know what happened."

Hon's pickup was in his driveway, so I walked across the road to see what he was doing and to get his version of the story. He was in his workshop, framing a picture.

"I heard you were in court," I said.

"Yeah," he answered as he taped the picture to the mat board. "I was called to testify as an expert witness."

He held the picture up to verify that he had centered it in the mat.

"Looks pretty good, doesn't it?" he said.

"Last year I worked with a committee to draft a proposal for the state legislature," he continued as he picked up a piece of glass and began to polish it. "Its purpose was to set uniform penalties for violations of our conservation laws, and to get the habitual offenders off the Bay. Now it's a law. If a waterman is convicted of three violations in one year, he loses his license."

He tilted the glass and squinted to see if any specs or lint remained.

"It's a good law, and honest watermen are happy to see it," he said. "It finally gives the Tidewater Fisheries the weapon they need to get the hogs off the bay, but their inspectors aren't enforcin' it properly."

He slipped the glass into the frame, then dropped the picture in behind it.

"A man doesn't normally work a boat by himself durin' the winter," he said. "We double up and share the expenses. Used to be, one man would tong and the other would cull, and then they'd swap places. They threw all their oysters in one pile, and when they sold at the dock, they took out the boat expenses and split the rest evenly. If they were caught with undersize oysters, they split the fine.

"With the new law, we had to change our way of workin'. The Watermen's Association instructed tongers to keep their oysters in separate piles, so the inspector can tell who is savin' the undersize ones and give the citation to him. In this case, though, the inspector found undersize oysters in the mate's pile, but gave the citation to the captain. We told him to take it to court, and the association would pay the lawyer.

"I was called to testify because I helped draft the law. I told the judge its purpose, and that the tongers had changed the way they worked just so the guilty ones could be identified."

He held the framed picture up to the light and examined it.

"Not good," he said. "I can still see some lint inside the glass."

He laid the frame face down on his bench and lifted the picture out.

"Well," he continued, "the judge found the captain guilty, anyway. He said the captain was responsible for anything that happened on the boat.

"So I spoke up. I asked the judge, 'If that inspector had found a dead man in the cabin and a smokin' gun on the oyster pile, would you try to find out who the murderer was, or just hang the captain?' I thought he was goin' to lock me up for

Hon dropping hydraulic tongs overboard

contempt."

He polished the glass again, then placed the picture back onto it.

"It's not over yet, though," he said. "We're appealin'. It's a new law, and the judge didn't understand the intent."

He held the picture up to examine it.

"Now it's right," he said. "I wouldn't put my name on it unless it's right."

He neatly wrapped a brown paper cover around the framed picture.

"Too many of those inspectors make a habit of treatin' us watermen like we were all criminals," he said as he taped the loose ends of the cover.

"I'll give you an example of what I mean by that. I was tongin' by myself one day when an inspector came aboard. To start with, that cuts down your catch because you miss a half hour's work anytime he checks your oysters. But you have to let him aboard, that's the law, so I just figure it's a part of my cost of doin' business.

"When you're tongin', you dump whatever you catch on your cullin' board. Then you cull. You toss the good oysters in a pile, and you sweep everything else back overboard. You can have undersize oysters on your cullin' board, and you're allowed a few in your pile, but not many. A man can't afford to stop and measure each oyster with a ruler, so the law allows you to have five percent undersize, no more.

"The inspector brings a tub and a cup on board with him. The tub holds a half bushel, the cup holds five percent of a bushel. He fills the tub and then measures every oyster in it. Any that are undersize, he drops into the cup. Then he fills the tub again. When he finishes cullin' that one, he better not have the cup full. If he does, he gives you a citation.

"When this inspector came aboard, he noticed a crack behind my cullin' board. So he took his shovel and went right under the cullin' board to the back of the pile to fill his tub. I couldn't complain, because it was my fault the cullin' board wasn't fit tight. I watched him measure that tub, and he nearly filled his cup. Then he picked up his shovel and started back under the cullin' board.

"I said, 'What are you doin' back there again?'

"He said he was goin' to full his tub.

"I told him he couldn't fill it twice from the same place.

"He told me he'd fill it from wherever he pleased.

"I quoted the law to him, and it says that he is supposed to take a representative sample. I told him if he took both tubs from the same place in the pile, that was not a representative sample, and he'd see me in court.

"He knew I was right. He grumbled and he eyed the pile for some more small oysters, but he couldn't spot any, so he filled the tub from the front. I watched him as he measured it, and he didn't find a one that was undersize. When he stepped back aboard his patrol boat, he told me he would get me the next time. Whenever that inspector showed up in the Tangier Sound after that, he came aboard and made me stop tongin' while he measured my oysters.

"A few weeks later I worked on a committee with the deputy director of the Department of Natural Resources. That's who the Tidewater Fisheries reports to. I told her about him harassin' me, and how I expected a citation if my oysters were undersized, but I also expected to be treated decently.

"I didn't see that inspector for weeks. When he finally came aboard again, he was like a different man. He even congratulated me for havin' a good cull.

"Trouble is, we don't often get the chance to talk to the

right people. The department heads and the legislators usually hear from the administrators and scientists, but not from us. Those people are paid for writin' their reports, but we can't afford to take time off from oysterin' to run up to Annapolis every few days, so the ones who set the policies only hear one side of the story. And right now, that side is blamin' most of the problems on the watermen."

The next day, I went to the shanty to look for Hon. I found him in the boat. He had stripped the stern deck off and was replacing the beams that braced the sides.

"She was twistin' in the waves," he said. "I needed to stiffen the sides before the boards all worked loose."

I mentioned an article that had appeared in the newspaper the day before. It quoted a marine biologist as saying that the Chesapeake could no longer stand being worked as common property, it should be divided into sections and cultivated by leaseholders.

"That's what those people are pushin'," he shouted as he slammed his fist down on the engine box. "If they had their way, the whole Bay would soon be fenced off into little plots with no trespassin' signs on the posts."

He was furious.

"They've been sayin' for years that the reason why there's a shortage of oysters and fish is because we watermen have caught too many. They claim we're just hunters and gatherers operatin' on common property, and we don't put anything back to replace what we've taken. They say that the only answer to the declinin' seafood problem is aquaculture. Any bottom that doesn't have oysters or clams they call barren, and say it should be leased for cultivation."

He picked up a board as he continued to talk.

"But they don't know what they're talkin' about. They sit in their offices and come up with all these theories, but they don't know the Bay.

"To start with," he said, as he fit a board into place and marked where he needed to cut it, "there's very little barren bottom. Where the oysters don't live, somethin' else does. We don't catch crabs on oyster rocks. If an acre of the Pocomoke Sound is leased for oysters, then we've lost an acre of the most productive crabbin' bottom in the world. If that acre was ideal for growin' oysters, they'd have grown there naturally."

Then he attacked the cultivation argument.

"The state of Washin'ton is always held up as an example of successful oyster cultivation," he said. "Over and over again, we hear how oysters should be grown in the Chesapeake the same as there. But the people who are tryin' to sell that line aren't tellin' the whole story. The truth is, Washin'ton wouldn't have an oyster industry without cultivation. The water's too cold. Oysters won't spawn in cold water, but they will grow in it once they've started. So, if Washin'ton wants oysters, they've got to spawn 'em artificially and then put 'em out to mature, but the Chesapeake is different. It has ideal conditions for natural oyster growth, and the most economical way to grow oysters is naturally.

"Somethin' else those people aren't tellin' is that we're not hunters and gatherers any more. We've been in the oyster cultivation business for years on the Chesapeake, and the watermen pay for it. Every bushel of oysters we sell is taxed to finance the shell plantin' program."

He carried the board he had marked to the band saw perched atop his engine box, and began to cut along the pencil line. As soon as the saw stopped whining, he resumed his argument.

"The Tidewater Fisheries directs the shell plantin'," he said. "They buy thousands of bushels of oyster shells every year and dump 'em overboard. When the oysters in the Bay spawn, the larva swim around for a few days lookin' for a place to attach. If they don't latch onto somethin', they die. That's why it's so important to have the shells overboard at the right time and in the right places. Trouble was, too many of the shells were dumped in the wrong places.

"Not only were they wastin' our money, we weren't gettin' the oysters we needed. We complained about it, so they told us to mark fifteen acres and they would plant shells there. Another waterman and I set the buoys usin' his boat. He has a Loran electronic position finder. Even when he's in a fog so thick he can't see his Samson post, his Loran tells him within a few feet of his exact position in the Bay. After we set the buoys, the Tidewater Fisheries people checked to see if we had marked off the fifteen acres accurately. They told me the buoys were pretty close, only about an acre off.

"Can you believe that? They were standin' on a rollin' boat usin' hand held instruments, sightin' water towers on shore and plottin' their position on a chart with a pencil, and they thought their locations were more accurate than ours.

"Well, those shells got a heavy strike of spat that year. It was no surprise to us, 'cause we watermen know where spat strike best. A waterman takes more samples in a day than a state biologist does in a year. When we're workin', we look at every oyster and every shell we pick up from the bottom. Every one of 'em is a sample that tells us if the spat are strikin' there.

"So, you see," he continued as he nailed the board into place, "we watermen have been payin' the oyster cultivation bill for years, but up until recently we haven't had any say at all as to how the money was spent. Still don't have much, and the results have been mighty disappointin'. So we're catchin' fewer oysters every year, and they're collectin' less taxes each year, and the plantin' program is in trouble for lack of funds."

He fit another board into place and scribed a line to match the curve of the stern.

"The reason why the funds are short isn't just because we aren't catchin' enough oysters," he said. "The Tidewater Fisheries collects the tax from the oyster packers, who take it out of the price they pay us, of course. I heard a Crisfield packer tell about how somebody had reported him for not payin' the taxes and he was fined. He was braggin' about how he could afford it, 'cause he had only been charged and fined once, but hadn't paid any oyster taxes at all that season. No wonder we're short of funds.

"We've appealed to the legislature for additional money to keep the plantin' program goin'. A lot of people criticized us for that, said we were becomin' too big a burden on the taxpayer. We got the money, though. The legislature appropriated a million dollars a year for five years."

He carried the board he had scribed to his bandsaw.

"A boat needs a little effort put into it once in a while," he said as he lined up his pencil mark with the blade, "but if you replace what wears out, you can keep it in good shape for a long time."

The bandsaw whined again, and Hon pressed the board against the blade. Halfway through the cut, the blade flew off the drive wheel. As he unbolted the saw's safety shield, he began to explain the practical side of the leasing controversy.

"Leasin' costs money," he said, "lots of it. First you have to buy the lease from the state. Then you have to plant oysters on it, and that costs plenty. Then you have to watch it, 'cause the Tidewater Fisheries tells us they don't have enough enforcement officers to police private beds. If you see somebody drudgin' your lease, you're supposed to call for 'em to send an officer. If they do, he'll be comin' in a patrol boat that runs about twenty miles an hour, so it'll be awhile before he gets there. Put me on a good bed of oysters and I can load my boat and be gone in less than thirty minutes, 'cause if I was stealin' oysters I wouldn't bother cullin', or abidin' by any other laws that would slow me down. So, even if you see somebody stealin' your oysters, the Tidewater Fisheries will never catch him. He'll keep comin' back until he steals all you have."

Hon slowly turned the saw's drive wheel and fed the blade onto it.

"Most of the potential leasin' bottom is way out from the land so you can't watch it," he said as he fit the shield back over the drive wheel, "but one waterman I know in the northern part of the county lives next to the river. His lease was right straight off the shore in front of his house. He looked out his livin' room window one day and saw somebody drudgin' his oysters, in plain view within hollerin' distance of his front door. His son grabbed up a rifle and shot at the boat. The state police arrested the boy for attempted murder.

"There's another problem with oyster leasin' that the people pushin' it ignore. They say a man who has a lease should be able to use any equipment he wants when he harvests his oysters, and he should be able to work whenever he wants. So a man could lease a few acres next to a natural rock that's been planted with our tax money. Then he could sneak across the line and drudge our oysters with his power boat when we're not allowed to be there and nobody would know it. He'd soon have all our oysters, and those scientists would be braggin' about how much more he was catchin' from his small leased acreage than we were catchin' from the natural rock. They'd hold him up as an example of how well their leasin' program was workin'.

"Average watermen just can't afford to buy those leases and keep 'em up," he continued. "If those scientists succeed in convincin' the legislature that leasin' is the best way to save our seafood, then I'm afraid the leases will be bought up mostly by big corporations, or by some wealthy religious cult whose followers work for a bowl of rice a day. Then they'll fence off thousands of acres and put their own patrols out there, and that will be the end of the independent watermen. Not only will our natural rocks be neglected, so much of the bottom will be planted in shells that we won't have any place left to crab. Then our boats won't be any value because there's no way to make a livin' on 'em, and no way to pay off the mortgages we took out to buy 'em, so we'll lose our homes as well as our jobs."

The saw whined again, and he pressed his board into it, being careful this time that he did not twist the blade. When he finished his cut and the saw stopped, he took up the common property argument.

"First I'll tell you the example those scientists use," he said. "Picture a big pasture, with a few cattle grazin' on it. The pasture is common property. Nobody owns it, but everybody who lives nearby can use it. People put a few cattle on it, and find out they can make a little money sellin' the cattle. If they can make a little money selling a few cattle, then they figure they can make more money sellin' more cattle. Since the pasture is common property and doesn't cost them more when they graze more cattle on it, they put as many cattle out there as they can find. Pretty soon, the cattle have eaten all the grass."

He hammered the board into place, then continued talking as though there had been no interruption.

"That example doesn't apply to the Bay," he said. "True, the oysters on public bottom are common property, and any waterman with a license can catch 'em, but there's where the similarity ends. The state has placed restrictions on us so we can't just keep catchin' more and more oysters to make more and more money. They've restricted the equipment we can use. That prevents us from catchin' many oysters in an hour. They've also restricted the hours we can work in a day, and the days we can work in a year. Then, just to make sure they didn't forget somethin', they limited the amount of oysters we can catch in a day."

He picked up another board, fit it into place, and scribed where he would cut it. Then he continued his argument.

"What they haven't limited is the number of watermen who can oyster. We watermen have proposed a way to do that. Don't issue a new license to anybody until they have served an apprenticeship, that's what we told 'em. That wouldn't be anything radical, lots of trades do it. We haven't heard anything back about that yet. They're not interested in our recommendations. As far as they're concerned, we're just ignorant watermen."

He carried the board to the saw, but he didn't turn it on until he finished what he had to say.

"The Bay is common property, though. I'll admit to that. It's a common dumpin' ground. It's where everything ends up that is poured into a sewer or sprayed on the ground anywhere within its watershed. That's a big area. It covers almost all of Maryland, almost all of Virginia, a large part of Pennsylvania, and some of Delaware and New York and West Virginia. The Tidewater Fisheries scientists don't consider pollution to be a problem, though. With my own ears, I heard one of them say in a meeting last month that the decline of fish and oysters in the Bay could not be traced to pollution by any substance. He was pushin' for more leasin', doin' his best to convince people that we watermen are the main problem. What he didn't say was that nine thousand acres of the Bay bottom have been leased to oyster growers for years, but only eleven percent of those acres are currently productive, because the oysters the growers planted *have died.*

"If leasin' worked as well as those scientists claim it will, we wouldn't be able to sail over those nine thousand acres without goin' aground on oysters."

He flipped the switch and the saw whined again. When he finished the cut, he hammered the final board into place and then jumped up and down on the deck.

"See," he said, "she's as stiff as a new one. That beam I put in might keep her another forty years."

"Good work," I told him.

"That was easy, compared to what I did last year," he said. "A drudge boat hit me while I was tied up to a dock at Deal Island, knocked my stem post loose. I pulled her up on the railway before she sank, cut the forward two feet off with a chain saw and put it back the next day. When I finished, the man who owned the railway offered me a job right there. I thought for a couple of days about takin' it, but then I found a good clump of oysters nobody else knew about."

He picked up the bandsaw and lugged it into the shanty. I followed along, carrying a handful of smaller tools.

"I was in the Pocomoke Sound by myself and for some reason, I don't know why, I decided to look around for a natural rock. All us watermen been workin' planted oysters so long I figured some might have grown without us noticin'. So I threw a piece of chain overboard and dragged it along behind. I hadn't gone far when it started to rattle, and I could tell it was on good oysters. I got so excited my heart began to pound and a big lump came up in my throat.

"I threw my anchor over, and I took a dip with my tongs. When I culled, every oyster was legal size. I didn't even bother cullin' after that. I just dipped 'em straight into the hold until I had about half my limit, then I went out to the planted oysters to finish the day. I did that so the other watermen wouldn't know what I'd found. The man I sold 'em to told me they were the best oysters he'd seen that year.

"I didn't go back for a few days, kept workin' the plants. Then I stopped off at my rock again for a few minutes. Those oysters were so thick I could have gotten my limit in an hour, but I didn't stay that long. That would have given away my secret. I kept that up for a while, just workin' my rock a half hour or so every few days, but eventually the other watermen figured out what I had found. They flocked over there and picked up every one. Now you can't find an oyster there, nothin' but muddy bottom.

"Can't blame anybody for takin' 'em all. The oysters were market size, and nobody workin' legal had made much more than expenses that year. The problem is, there's not enough oysters out there. Even if there were more, there's no entry limit, so anybody with a boat and a set of tongs can go catch 'em. During the first part of the season, when the weather is good and the new growth is thick, a whole lot of people who don't normally oyster show up. There'll be chicken farmers and auto mechanics and drunks just lookin' to make enough money to keep 'em in booze during the cold weather. Everybody does well for a little while, but then the oysters start to give out. That's when all but the true watermen go ashore. We stay out there strugglin' through the cold weather and the nor'westers to try to meet expenses until crabbin' begins.

"Right now, the chicken farmers and mechanics and drunks have just as much right to the oysters as the full time watermen, and that sounds fair to me, as long as there's enough to go around. But now, with too many people chasin' too few oysters, we're goin' to have to tell some people they can't work on the natural rocks anymore. We can't pick 'em randomly, though, it's got to be the ones who are doin' it as a sideline. How could you tell a Smith Islander he can't oyster any more? He's got no other way to earn a livin'.

"When I found that natural rock," he continued, "I was draggin' where I knew the conditions were right. I can't tell you how that rock started. Maybe a fish rooted up a clam in the spring and ate it, and left the shell layin' on the bottom. Larva from an oyster miles away drifted over with the current and latched onto the shell. Maybe ten or more latched on and became spat, because the shell was clean. When they grew, they pushed each other apart and broke off the shell, and scattered about there on the bottom, pickin' up more larva. Pretty soon, those ten oysters became a hundred, and they became a thousand, and then ten thousand. Within a few years, they could have numbered in the millions.

"With the proper conditions, oysters multiply mighty fast, and the Chesapeake used to have those conditions. Now, the beds are buried under silt and algae covers everything in the water, so the few larva that aren't killed by pollution can't find a hard surface to catch ahold. If an oyster somehow manages to get started, it stands a good chance of dyin' from poor water quality, or it's so weakened that a disease comes along and kills it.

"If more of the research budget was spent on solvin' those problems," he said, "then we'd have a lot more oysters."

"Want to go to a wildfowl art show tomorrow?" Hon asked, abruptly changing the topic. "I've rented a booth."

"Sure," I replied.

I knew I wouldn't want to stay all day, so I didn't go along with him in the morning. Instead, I drove to the Salisbury Civic Center about noon. The show was divided into two parts. The artists and their exhibits were in the main auditorium. There I found carvings of swimming geese and flying ducks, and one of an egret standing among tall rushes with a velvet backdrop. The commercial booths were in a separate room from the artist's exhibits. It was smaller than the main auditorium, but still large enough to hold two basketball courts. I found Hon's booth under one of the backboards.

As I squeezed through the crowd, I heard someone call my name. It was Jack Andrews, a friend from Crisfield whom I had not seen for more than twenty years. During the glory days of the Bay seafood industry, his grandfather owned the biggest blacksmith shop in town. Jack still tinkered in the trade as a hobby, and had become one of the better known makers of knives for wood carvers. His booth was next to Hon's.

Jack pulled an extra chair into his booth. I sat and talked with him during the lulls while Hon sliced away at a block of wood with a knife Jack had loaned him. He was carving a bird, his first. For a model he was using a rubber duck, the kind children play with in a bathtub.

Jack and Hon had both been on duty continuously since early morning. Jack suggested that Hon look after the two booths for about thirty minutes while he took a break. When he came back, he would return the favor. Hon said that sounded like a good idea, so Jack disappeared in the crowd.

Shortly after he walked away, a man stopped in front of his booth and began examining the knives.

"Can I help you?" Hon offered.

"What kind of steel are these knives made from?"

I knew Hon couldn't answer that, but he didn't hesitate with his response.

"Do you know much about steel?"

"No," the man replied.

"Then why'd you ask?"

The next day I walked across the road to Hon's shop to see if he had sold much at the show.

"I did all right," he said. "I sold twelve framed prints and about twice that many unframed. And I sold that little duck for twenty-five dollars."

He began to dig through a cardboard box filled with papers on the floor beside his desk. "There's somethin' in here I want to show you," he said. "Here it is."

He lifted out a thick document that looked like a government report. He flipped the pages until he came to a chart that was shaded to show where oysters in the Bay had grown naturally through the years. The lightest shading indicated the original area, the darkest shading indicated the most recent years. The chart showed that the natural oyster growth, which once covered most of the Maryland portion of the Bay, had receded to only a small area along the Eastern Shore.

"Look," he said as he traced his finger along the map from the Susquehanna River southward, "this is where the oysters disappeared first, near the western shoreline. This is where most of the people live, where you will find most of the city sewers and the farms."

Then he moved his finger to the eastern side of the Bay, to the Tangier Sound and the waters adjacent to it.

"This is where the best natural oyster growth in the Bay still occurs, and this is where the fishin' has always been the heaviest. If those scientists are right, and the only reason why we don't have a good natural set of oysters now is that we've overfished them and caught up the brood stock, why are they here?

"The legislature banned the catchin' of shad years ago," he said. "Those scientists claimed we were depletin' the brood stock, not leavin' enough to replenish the population, just like they're now sayin' about oysters. But the ban didn't fix the problem. The sad truth is, if we never catch another shad or rockfish or oyster, they'll still disappear like the eel grass unless the water quality improves. Those scientists show up at the legislature with their fancy charts and statistics, and they bedazzle everybody with such big words nobody knows what they're talkin' about. They sound so convincin' they're hard to argue against. But how much can you trust their figures when they can't even tell you how many oysters are caught in a year? They arrive at their estimates from the number of bushels that the oyster packers have reported for taxes. You can multiply the number of watermen on the Bay by the bushels each has to catch just to pay his expenses, and it's obvious that their figures are way below the true catch.

"And the Tidewater Fisheries inspectors think that we watermen are the only pirates on the Bay."

Chapter 10
A Time of Fighting Back

"Hon might get a state job," Margaret said. "They advertised an opening in the oyster planting program, and he applied. He took the test, and I'm sure he did well on it. He certainly has the experience to qualify."

This sounded promising to me, so I walked across the road to look for him. I found him in the workshop, typing a letter.

"Margaret tells me you applied for a state job," I said. "What do you figure your chances are?"

"I have a lot of friends in the state government now," he said, "and one of them told me I was the most qualified candidate. He said if I just kept quiet for awhile and convinced them I'd be a team player, the job would be mine."

"That's encouraging," I said. "What are you typing?"

"A letter to the governor. You won't believe what the Tidewater Fisheries scientists are tryin' to do with that million dollars that was appropriated for plantin' oysters this year. They want to use it to buy an old factory building. I'm tellin' him how foolish that is, and copyin' all the legislators."

"There goes your job."

"I don't care. If it would mean I had to stand by and watch while they mismanage the oyster program like that, then I don't want it. They can't pay me enough money to keep me quiet."

"Why do they want the old factory?"

"For an oyster hatchery. Trouble is, they already have one oyster hatchery, and it's next to useless. There's no good reason for 'em to take our shell plantin' money for another one."

"I didn't know there was an oyster hatchery on the Bay," I said.

"You want to see it? It's on Deal Island, we can drive there in forty minutes."

Hon knew that Laura Ritter, the editor of the *Crisfield Times*, was concerned about the predicament of the watermen, and was especially interested in exploring the effectiveness of the state programs to restore the seafood industry in the Bay. We knew she could get into the hatchery more easily than we could, so we stopped by the *Times* office and there we found her, a crusading five foot two inch whirlwind in blue jeans.

"Yes, I'd like to visit the hatchery," she said. "I've been eager to see it ever since this article appeared in the *Waterman's Gazette.*"

She flipped through the pages of the September issue. "Here it is," she said as she spread the magazine out on her desk for us to read.

Hon and I read the article. It stated that the reason for purchasing the factory and converting it to an oyster hatchery "...is because of the technical feasibility and excellent opportunity this situation affords the state of Maryland. This facility can be obtained at a minimal cost, and converted into an extremely efficient, high volume production unit with the state of the art technology that exists now...."

"Looks to me like they'll soon use the shell planting money to buy that factory unless somebody comes up with a serious objection," Laura said.

The Deal Island oyster hatchery was in a new concrete block building beside the water, close to the docks where the skipjacks were tied. The side door wasn't locked, so we walked in. The entire hatchery spread out before us, all in one neat, well organized room. A wide aisle ran down the center of the building. On each side of it, a row of white tubs stood on legs that brought them to waist height. Each tub was about four feet wide, eight feet long, and twelve inches deep, and most of them were filled with wire baskets leveled off with oyster shells. Two men at the far end of the building were busy scrubbing tubs. One of them put down his brush and walked toward us.

"I'm the hatchery manager," he said as he held out his hand.

We introduced ourselves, and Laura explained to him why she was interested in seeing the hatchery operation. She told him how important oysters were to Crisfield, and that her readers wanted to know what was being done to bring them back. The manager said he would be happy to explain the complete process.

He pointed toward a row of fiberglass cylinders to our left, each about three feet in diameter and four feet high. He told us that he fills these vats with water he has filtered to remove predators. Then he pours in oyster larva that the Department of Natural Resources laboratory sends to him. He told us that because of the high concentration of larva in the vats, he continually pumps a fresh supply of filtered water from the harbor and circulates it through them. He also adds algae to the vats as a food supplement. He receives the algae from the laboratory as a paste and blends it with water before pouring it into the vats.

While the larva mature, the manager and his helper shovel oyster shells into half bushel wire baskets, wash them with a high pressure hose, and place the baskets into the tanks. After the larva have been in the vats for ten days, they are ready to set. At that time, the manager fills the tanks with filtered water and releases the larva so they can attach to the shells.

In the clear water, the larva appear as tiny specks. He watches closely to see when they set on the shells, which may take days. While he waits for the set, he circulates filtered water through the tubs and feeds the larva, just as he did when they were in the vats.

Once the larva have set and become spat, the manager and his helper spend most of their time keeping the tubs clean so the spat will not be smothered by silt. They drain the tubs daily, lift out the baskets of shells, scrub the tubs, put the baskets of shells back, and run fresh harbor water over them. This is what they were doing when we walked in, and the helper was still busy at it.

The manager picked an oyster shell from one of the baskets. He told us that these spat had recently set, and if we looked closely, we could see them.

"I see something on the shell that looks like little specks of pepper," Laura said.

"They are the spat," he told her.

We followed him to the far end of the building. Here, he showed us a shell from another tub. Miniature oysters were clustered all over it. He told us that these spat had been set for about three weeks longer than the ones we just looked at. Laura and I were amazed at how large they had grown.

Laura asked, "Are those little oysters too crowded on the shell?"

The manager told her that when the shells are spread out on the bottom of the Bay, the oysters would grow and push against each other until most of them broke off. By that time they should be able to survive on their own, whether they remained attached to a shell or not.

"There's no way to control the distribution of spat on the shells," he said. "We put enough larva in the tubs so the shells will have plenty of spat. Sometimes we set more than six thousand spat per bushel of shells, but that is exceptional. Normally we get much less."

Laura asked, "How many oysters in a bushel?"

"About three hundred fifty."

Laura scribbled briefly in her notebook.

"That's about seventeen bushels of oysters from one bushel of these shells," she said.

"If they all live."

The manager told us that the spat he had just shown us were almost hardy enough that they no longer needed the water to be filtered. This meant he could soon remove them from the tubs and put them in the harbor. He led us out to the docks beside the hatchery and showed us how he ties a rope to each basket and lowers it into the harbor. Here the young oysters will hang, suspended just below the water's surface and cleansed by the changing tides until they are ready to plant.

Laura asked him, "Do you try to produce oysters with specific characteristics, like resistance to diseases."

"No," he said. "We do not breed for any specific characteristics. I take whatever larva the laboratory sends and set spat. I have never been instructed to segregate the spat produced by any particular batch of larva. When the oysters are planted, nobody knows which ones came from which larva."

"What is the total production of this hatchery during a year?"

"Three hundred bushels," he said. "Our greatest limitation is time. We have to wash the shells to prepare them for the larva to set, and then wash them every day as long as they are in the tanks."

We thanked him for showing us around the hatchery and started the drive back to Crisfield. On the way, Laura pulled out her note pad and began discussing with us what she had seen.

"Hon," she said, "you know more about the oyster industry than I do. Tell me if that manager is doing a good job."

"He's doin' a good job. He's obviously conscientious and he works hard."

"I can't believe you said that. You've been so critical of the Tidewater Fisheries getting into the oyster hatchery business."

"Get your pencil out," Hon said. "How much do you think the state spends a year on that hatchery?"

"That would include building, equipment, docks, and electricity for pumps and lights," she said.

"And salaries and benefits for two men. The state spends a lot on employee benefits."

"Of course, I know that."

"And don't forget the larva and algae paste that come from the lab. State employees are producin' that, too."

Laura scratched in her notebook, and then she looked up. "At least sixty thousand dollars a year," she said.

"Now," Hon said, "divide that by the number of bushels they produce in a year."

"Sixty thousand divided by three hundred, that's two hundred."

"Those oysters cost two hundred dollars a bushel!"

"But Hon, they're just baby oysters. They grow up and then they'll fill a lot more bushels."

"Look in your notes. How many bushels of oysters did you figure we would get from one bushel of those shells?"

Laura flipped back a couple of pages, then scratched in her notebook again.

"As many as seventeen, if they all live," she said.

"Seventeen is a lot higher than the average, but you can use that figure if you want. Only one third of them will live to maturity, though. You've got the pencil. Figure out how much each of those bushels of marketable oysters would cost."

"Let's see," Laura said. "I'd divide the two hundred dollars by one third of the seventeen bushels, wouldn't I?"

"That's right. What's the answer?"

"Wait a minute. I need my calculator for that."

She punched in the numbers. "Thirty-five dollars and twenty-nine cents a bushel," she said.

"Last year," Hon said, "oysters sold for nine dollars a bushel at the dock. We've already lost over twenty-six dollars on each bushel before we pay the man who catches them."

"Doesn't make much sense to grow oysters that way," Laura said, "but what else can they do?"

"Plant shells with the money," he said. "We can spread shells on a rock for as little as twenty-five cents a bushel. One good natural spat strike in the Bay would produce more oysters in a year than a hundred hatcheries will in a lifetime. The problem is not with the manager. The problem is with the process. There's just no sense in spendin' one million dollars of our shell plantin' money on a hatchery 'til those scientists prove they can grow oysters for a lot less than two hundred dollars a bushel."

"That's depressing," Laura said. "Must it cost so much to grow oysters in a hatchery?"

"Let's ask Max," Hon said.

181

"Who's Max?"

"He has a hatchery near Fairmount."

"There's another hatchery? Why haven't I heard about it?"

"Max doesn't get much publicity, but he's growin' oysters."

We turned off the highway at the Fairmount sign and headed toward the Bay. Beyond the village, far down a narrow road that meandered along the highest ground of a marsh, we found Max's hatchery. It wasn't very impressive, just a rusty metal shed beside a tidal creek. As we stepped out of the car, a pickup truck crunched to a stop beside us on the oyster shell lane.

"Here's Max now," Hon said.

A thin, energetic looking man in a bathing suit hopped out. He was dripping wet.

"Be with you shortly," he said. "Let me put some pants on before the mosquitoes eat me up."

In a little more than a minute, he popped back out the door wearing jeans and a loose fitting shirt. Hon introduced Laura and me, and asked Max if he would mind explaining his operation to us.

Max began by showing us the tumbler he made from steel rods and an old electric motor. He and his wife shovel shells into it and wash them with high pressure jets as the basket revolves. Then they dump the shells from the tumbler into mesh bags that hold a half bushel each. Max told us that washing the shells increased the percent of larva that attached to them, but it took more of his time than any other task in the hatchery process. The tumbler was his own invention, and had improved his efficiency considerably.

Max led us into his shed. Just inside the door were his

larva vats, very similar to the ones we had seen at the Tidewater Fisheries hatchery. Behind the vats were several fiberglass cylinders about the size of water heaters. Each was filled with a green liquid, each a slightly different shade. I asked him what they held.

"Algae," he replied, "supplemental food for the larva."

"You grow your own algae?"

"Sure, that isn't difficult at all. The pond out back of the shed has no outlet, so it can't flush with the tide. Algae grows naturally in it. I pump water from the pond, filter the predators out, and fill these cylinders. I feed the algae until it's the proper color, then I pump it into the larva vats."

"How do you know what the proper color is?"

"Trial and error. When you live with it long enough, you learn."

Beyond the vats and cylinders were the tubs where Max set his spat. Most of his tubs were filled with motionless water and bags of shells. Laura asked him why the water wasn't circulating.

"The spat don't need water to be circulating all the time," Max said. "I kept reducing the time I pumped water into them until I got down to an hour a day. That seems to produce results as good as if I ran the pumps continuously. It saves wear on the pumps, it saves twenty-three hours of electricity a day, and the tanks stay cleaner because I don't pump as much sediment into them."

Laura observed, "That should mean you don't have to scrub the tanks very often."

"I don't scrub them at all, except when I'm getting ready to put a batch of fresh shells in."

"That must save you a lot of time."

"Yes, I use the time to wash more shells. The limit to my

production is the amount of shells I can wash."

Laura asked, "Where do you get your larva?"

"I spawn it myself. I can start with three bushels of oysters and spawn all the larva I need for the whole year."

Laura scribbled on her note pad.

"Since you spawn them yourself," she said, "do you try to develop oysters with certain characteristics?"

"Interesting you brought that up," Max replied. "Just a few weeks ago, I asked a state scientist if they were attempting to breed a disease resistant oyster, and he told me it wasn't possible. He said oysters don't have the ability to develop natural resistance, but I know he's wrong. A few years ago, some bars near here were just about wiped out by disease, only a few oysters survived. A waterman brought me a couple of bushels because he was certain they were disease resistant, and he asked if I could grow more from them. Some day, I hope we'll be able to build up rocks of disease resistant oysters, but it's too early to tell.

"I grow oysters for other characteristics, too. Those from deep water don't do well in marshy creeks, and those from shallow water don't seem to do well when you move them deep. If someone wants to plant oysters in deep water, I spawn them from ones I take from deep water. If someone wants to plant oysters in creeks, I spawn them from creek oysters. When I saw you drive up here, I was breaking oysters loose under the bridge. I'm hoping I can breed some that will grow right up in a marsh.

"I would like to try to breed more oysters for specific conditions," Max said, "but I don't have much time to spend at it. I'm too busy washing shells."

Laura asked, "How much do you charge for a bushel of shells that you've set spat on?"

"I charge three dollars and fifty cents for enough spat to grow one bushel of marketable oysters," Max said. "I figure three hundred fifty will survive to marketable size from a thousand spat, and that's a bushel."

Laura scribbled in her notebook. Then she asked Max what he considered to be the problem with the oyster industry today.

"The watermen are catching too many," he said.

"You're wrong!" Hon replied emphatically. "There aren't enough new ones growin', that's the problem. Anyway, if you stopped watermen from catchin' 'em, what good would they be?"

"Filtration," Max said. "They filter the water."

"I hadn't looked at it that way," Hon said. "An average size oyster does filter twenty-five gallons of water a day. But you can't ask watermen to stop catchin' 'em for that."

"A bushel filters close to ten thousand gallons a day," Max said, "and a lot more than that in warm weather. Enough oysters in the Bay would help clean up some of the pollution, especially the algae growth."

Laura stopped scribbling in her notebook long enough to ask, "Can't we have our cake and eat it too? I mean, if somebody doesn't catch the oysters they'll eventually die of old age, and that seems a waste, much as I like to eat them."

"Let me restate my position," Max said. "One of the problems with the oyster industry in the Bay is that we just don't have enough oysters to filter the water, so the accumulating algae is smothering the oysters and the other sea life. I didn't mean to say we should get rid of the watermen. I'm just saying we need more oysters. I don't care if the watermen catch twenty million bushels a year, as long as we have plenty left."

"Now, I'll agree with you," Hon said. "I'd like to see us catch a lot more, too, but this Bay'll never grow that many. We only caught fifteen million bushels in the peak year, and that was workin' virgin beds in pristine waters."

"Twenty million may be possible," Max said. "I suspect the food supply originally limited the number of oysters the Bay could grow. Oysters feed on algae, and there's a lot more of it in the water now."

Hon took off his glasses and wiped them on his shirt tail. "You make a lot of sense," he said.

"I just don't understand the reason for the difference between the two hatcheries," Laura said as we were driving back. "The state produces oysters for thirty-five dollars a bushel, but Max charges three dollars fifty cents. Why is the state ten times more expensive?"

"Here's the way I look at it," Hon said. "The state hatchery manager is bound by procedures and fundin' that he can't control. Come back in ten years and he'll still be growin' his three hundred bushels, but Max will find a way to increase his production and bring down his cost per bushel every year. Somethin' else you have to consider, you can't hire a man and expect him to work as hard as Max."

"Max doesn't talk like a waterman, but he reminds me of one," Laura said. "He's so resourceful."

"He grew up on a farm," Hon replied, "but he was born to be a waterman. Very rare for anybody to come from ashore and stick with it like he has."

"Instead of spending a million dollars for a hatchery and then growing such expensive oysters in it," Laura asked, "why doesn't the Tidewater Fisheries just buy them from Max?"

"We'd all be better off," Hon replied.

"Wait a minute," Laura said as she flipped back through the pages of her notebook. "Here it is. You said you could plant shells for twenty-five cents a bushel. If you can plant them so cheaply, why do we need a hatchery at all?"

"We can use a hatchery, but not for the reason the state gives. I've talked with Max before. He says he can breed larger, faster growin' oysters. We watermen keep oysters as soon as they reach three inches. That means we take the fast growers and leave the runts in the water. So the natural rocks are being replenished by the spawn of oysters so inferior that many may never grow to a marketable size. The state needs to be spendin' some of our oyster tax money to buy superior spat and spread 'em on our natural rocks to improve the quality of the spawn."

"I can see a good story coming out of this," Laura said as she scribbled in her notebook again. "Can Max supply enough oysters to do any good?"

"Max can supply enough larva to do a lot of good. He doesn't have to set the spat on the shells. Watermen can do that, and there are thousands of us. We already have most of the equipment we need. Our sheddin' floats would make good tanks for settin' spat. We could buy larva from Max and set the spat in our spare time at the shanty.

"This would give us an additional income, and we sure need it. We could sell the spat to the state or to lease holders, or we'd use 'em to start our own leases if we could find a way to protect 'em.

"Or, if those scientists could use their research money to figure out how to tell exactly when larva is ready to attach, then we could spread shell and lay the larva on 'em and know they will set before the tide carries 'em off. That way, we could grow a lot of oysters, and mighty cheap."

Cold weather came and the oyster season began, but Hon stayed home. He wanted to go, he just couldn't. His right leg had been bothering him for almost a year, and finally became so painful he couldn't stand on it for more than a few minutes at a time. I found him sitting at the desk in his shop with his leg propped up on a chair. He was cutting circles out of a piece of cardboard with his scissors.

"The doctor told me I should rest it," he said. "I asked him how I was goin' to make a livin'. He told me I had to figure that part out myself."

I asked how the art and picture framing business was going. He said it was picking up. He hoped he would make enough money at it to keep him through Christmas. That was all he needed, because he had a contract to start work with a team of doctors from Johns Hopkins University in January. They were studying the effects of ultraviolet radiation on human health, and had chosen to survey the watermen because their exposure to the sun is so great.

"What can you do to help them?" I asked.

"I'm their contact with the watermen," he said. "It takes a waterman to work with watermen, you know.

"Maybe the Tidewater Fisheries will learn that some-day," he continued, "and pay a few watermen to be their contacts. That would save a lot of problems, like when they were tryin' to decide where to build a fishin' reef. They scheduled a hearin', and invited us watermen to it. When they held up their charts to show us where the reef was goin', we told 'em it was in the wrong place. It was right in the middle of a good crabbin' bottom. So they told us they'd pick another place, and they went back to Annapolis. When they scheduled the next hearin', they didn't invite any watermen. They only invited the sport fishin' captains. Those guys didn't care where the reef was put, because they don't crab. But we found out about it, so we showed up. Well, they'd put the reef in a worse place than the first time, and we told 'em so.

"The Tidewater Fisheries people asked us where we would put it. We recommended a spot in the Tangier Sound. Everybody was happy with it, so they said that's where the reef would go. Then they asked if we had any more questions.

"I told 'em I had one. I asked if it wouldn't have been easier to have held this meetin' first?

"Oh," he said as he put his scissors down. "You don't know about the results of our court case, the one where the Tidewater Fisheries inspector gave the citation to the boat captain. In the appeal, our attorney used pretty much the same argument that almost got me in trouble, that if the mate killed somebody you wouldn't hang the captain. The judge agreed that one man shouldn't be penalized when another man was obviously guilty. He ruled in our favor.

"And our shell plantin' money wasn't used to buy that factory, either. We're beginnin' to win some of the battles now. I gotta get ready for the big one, though. We're goin' to fight to stop the Bay from bein' leased. I know what's goin' to happen. Those scientists will stand up before the legislature with all their charts and statistics and big words. They'll show how the oyster catch has been in a steady decline, and they'll sing their old chorus about how leasin' is all that's needed to reverse the trend. But they won't mention any of the problems with leasin', so that's when I'll speak up, and I've got a new weapon to help me fight 'em this year."

"What's that?"

"I'll show you," he said.

He picked up the three circular disks he had cut out of cardboard. He laid the largest on a scrap of plywood, placed the middle sized one over it, and placed the smallest over the other two. He then drove a nail through the disks, right at the center point, pinning them to the plywood.

"See," he said, "I've got a word wheel."

I peered at the disks more closely. He had written words around the rim of each, big words that looked terribly technical.

"All I do is spin the wheels," he said, "and wherever they stop, I line up three words."

He spun the disks, lined up three words, and read them.

"Hydrological resource degeneration," he said.

He spun the disks again.

"Deoxygenated marine dehabilitation. Now I can use big words like a Tidewater Fisheries scientist, and mine make just as much sense."

Chapter 11
A Time of Looking Ahead

I was half way across Hon's front yard when I heard the calls coming from high overhead. I looked up into the darkening sky of the late afternoon to see a long string of big birds with outstretched necks flying in formation, each one slightly behind and to the left of the one ahead. They appeared to be geese, with their long necks stretched out ahead of them, but they didn't sound like geese.

"Swan," Hon said, "about a hundred of 'em, headed for the Pocomoke Sound."

I had been watching the birds so intently I did not notice him come out the front door. With him was Bill Goldsborough, staff scientist for the Chesapeake Bay Foundation, a nonprofit organization that has been very effective at educating the public concerning the deteriorating condition of the Bay environment.

"Come on over to the shop," Hon said. "I was about to show Bill some new picture framin' equipment I bought today."

I followed Hon and Bill between two stacks of rusted crab pots and through the back door.

"Let me show you how this works," Hon said as he clamped a picture framing mat board onto his work bench, adjusted the blade of his new cutter, and turned the crank one revolution.

"See how perfect the cut is," he said as he handed the mat to Bill. "Not only does it save me a lot of time, it also makes a perfect oval."

Hon reached into a box on the shelf behind the mat cutter and pulled out a print of a duck. He took the mat board back from Bill, taped the print behind it, and held it up for us to see.

"That's very nice," Bill said.

"Here, you can have it," Hon said as he handed it to Bill.

"Thanks, I'll hang it in my office."

"Don't you want me to frame it for you? I only charge twenty-five dollars."

"The reason I came to see you," Bill said as he began to shuffle through Hon's picture molding samples, "is to collect some information about the effects of the current water quality on Bay fisheries. Do many of your crabs die in the pots?"

"No," Hon responded, "but that's because I work in the Pocomoke Sound. Anybody who sets pots in the main Bay can expect to bring up dead crabs, though. And a lot more die before they get to the market."

"That sounds like anoxia," Bill said as he handed Hon the molding of his choice, "reduced levels of dissolved oxygen in the water. Anything it doesn't kill, it weakens."

"Sometimes a potter will be catchin' twenty bushels a day," Hon said as he carried a strip of molding across the room to his workbench. "All of a sudden, he gets a fifty bushel day. Next day he goes out lookin' for another big haul, but all he finds are dead crabs. They were runnin' to stay ahead of the bad water."

"Crabs will move to avoid anoxia," Bill said, "but oysters can't. When it occurs over a bar, it can kill every one there."

"There's probably not an oyster alive in the whole state of Maryland in water deeper than twenty feet," Hon said as he sliced off a length of molding. His molding shear was shiny new. Every time he had spare money, he now spent it on framing equipment instead of crab pots.

"Oxygen deficiency used to be found mostly in water deeper than forty feet, but it's becoming much more widespread," Bill said. "Many Bay scientists believe it is killing fish and crabs, and especially oysters. But, and I know this sounds incredible to you, Hon, there is currently no scientific documentation that anoxia has any adverse impact on living marine resources."

"Some things just require common sense," Hon grunted. "How long do you think an oyster can hold its breath?"

"I plan to set a string of crab pots this summer," Bill continued. "I'll run them from shallow water out to the deep. I'll fish them every day, and when I do, I'll take a water sample from the same depth as each pot. Then I'll try to correlate the low oxygen levels with the incidence of dead crabs."

"Look how these corners fit together," Hon said as he laid four pieces of molding onto his workbench. "I used to cut my frames with a saw, but this shear is much more precise. Whatever you do nowadays, you gotta have good equipment."

Then he looked up at Bill. "Suppose the dead water came in with the tide at night, but was gone next mornin'. It would kill all the crabs in your pots, but how could you prove it?"

"The sampling process can be slow," Bill said. "Conclusive proof usually takes a long time."

"You could take years to complete that study." Hon was talking faster, like he does when his temper begins to rise. "Meanwhile, my crabs have all died and I'm out of business. If you guys had to make a livin' from what you catch in those pots, you'd be in a lot more of a hurry."

"Wait a minute, Hon. Besides having to deal with you watermen, Bay scientists have to work with two state legislatures and about a dozen federal and state agencies. Everybody says they want the Bay cleaned up, but it is very expensive and time consuming to sort out the processes of a body of water like the Chesapeake. This is the largest estuary in North America, and an estuary is very complex by nature. Unfortunately, it is also a very popular place for people to live, and as the population density increases, we find our situation becoming worse, because the problems are accumulating much faster than the answers."

"And us watermen are bein' forced off the Bay," Hon snapped.

"Watermen are the first ones to feel the pinch," Bill acknowledged. "I know they are indicators of Bay conditions, and that the decline of the seafood industry should be a signal that the Chesapeake has serious problems."

"We watermen are just as much an indicator of the Bay's health as the fish and the oysters and the eel grass," Hon said, "maybe even better, 'cause we're the only indicator that complains."

"There's a benefit to that," Bill replied. "We don't know the other indicators are hurting until they die. You mentioned eel grass, how is it doing around here? Dying aquatic grass is usually associated with the same factors that lead to anoxia."

"Eel grass is beginnin' to come back to the Pocomoke," Hon said. "This has been a dry year, though, and that seems to make a difference. I'd say the grass will die off again next year if we have more rain."

"That's probably true," Bill said. "Rainy years seem to be worse for the aquatic grasses and for the general health of the Bay because of the increase in runoff."

Bill went on to explain the major cause of anoxia and dying aquatic vegetation. "Nutrients enter the Bay from many sources," he said, "especially from sewer outflows and rainfall runoff. Since nutrients act as fertilizer, people tend to think the more that goes into the Bay the more productive the Bay will be. Unfortunately, most of this added productivity has been in the form of algae, because it multiplies more rapidly than other aquatic plants. As the nutrients increase, the algae population explodes to consume it.

"The multiplying algae has a very short life span, so although its population may be expanding rapidly, vast amounts of it are dying at the same time. Dead algae cells are decomposed by bacteria, and this process reduces the level of dissolved oxygen in the water. The thicker and more widespread the algae growth, the lower the oxygen concentration, until there is no oxygen left. That is what is causing our anoxia."

"And that's one reason why the oysters are dying and fish are about gone," Hon said.

"Anoxia has another problem associated with it. Even though the dissolved oxygen returns to the water at a later time, the habitat is severely damaged. In recent years, algae has become so thick in many portions of the Bay it clouds the water to the point that sunlight will not penetrate it. When this occurs, the submerged aquatic vegetation dies, because it cannot survive without sunlight. With the submerged aquatic vegetation gone, small fish and molting crabs that migrate into the area cannot find a place to hide, and waterfowl have nothing to eat."

"That's just what I've seen happen."

"We used to think of the Bay as a big sewer," Bill continued, "pour anything in and it would flow out to sea. We now know this is not true. Much of what we pour into the Bay stays there. The excess nutrients that result in anoxia constitute the most apparent problem today, but toxic substances are potentially more dangerous. They tend to bind to suspended sediment, which eventually settles.

"The Bay has its own circulation pattern, which we have just recently begun to understand. Fresh water, which is lighter than salt water, runs off the land and flows as a layer along the surface toward the ocean. The heavier salt water also flows as a layer along the bottom, but it moves from the ocean inward toward the upper part of the Bay and eventually mixes with the fresh. As sediment settles, it falls to the inward flow, so it never leaves the Bay. The toxicants that are carried by this sediment become trapped in the Bay, and accumulate on the bottom.

"Some of these toxicants are absorbed by microscopic plants and animals, which are eaten by small fish, which are in turn eaten by larger fish. The more small fish a large one eats, the more toxicants accumulate in its tissues. Then, the large fish are caught and eaten by humans. Accumulated toxicants can be a severe problem. In some areas of the Bay, they already are."

"But not here," Hon said.

"Not yet. The lower Eastern Shore has very few local sources of toxicants, because it has little industry and few people."

"I remember seein' a special on TV about toxic wastes," Hon said. "A man and his wife were bein' interviewed as they walked along the seashore on the coast of England. They described how the wastes that were discharged into the water eventually washed up onto the shore, dried, and were blown inland by the sea breezes as dust to cover the streets and playgrounds and the furniture in their homes. This couple raised ducks, and their ducklin's were deformed. They wondered how much longer before their children would be born deformed, too."

"We don't have a condition anywhere near that bad," Bill said.

"You told me the toxicants were accumulatin', so it's bound to get worse."

"True. Unfortunately, it's hard to control the illegal discharge of toxic substances under our present regulatory system, and a lot of toxicants are even being discharged legally. This is frightening. We have a history in this country of not being concerned with a problem until the effects are recognized and documented, and liability is proven by some lengthy process. This can result in disastrous environmental and health problems before any corrective actions are attempted."

"Do you know what I think is our greatest problem?" Hon said.

"What's that?"

"The Bay looks too clean. Take somebody out on a boat and they come back to shore happy. They don't see any problem. Reminds me of the time I was in an airplane and the pilot pointed out that we were passin' over a hurricane. The passengers were tellin' each other how pretty it was with all those fluffy, white clouds. But I'd been through a hurricane, so I knew that what was goin' on along the ground wasn't pretty at all.

"While I'm out there on the Bay tryin' to catch enough to pay my expenses and feed my family, somebody needs to be tellin' people what's happenin' under the surface. Somebody needs to be tellin' the real reason why the shad and the rockfish have all but disappeared, and why the oysters are disappearin', and why we watermen are goin' to disappear along with 'em."

"You've been doing a good job of that," Bill said. "I try to get to every legislative hearing that concerns the Bay

197

fisheries, and you're usually there, telling the watermen's side of the story."

"I drove to Annapolis twenty-one times last year, all at my own expense. Nobody pays me a salary for goin' there, and I miss a day's work every trip. I just can't afford to keep that up. Somebody else is goin' to have to tell the watermen's story from now on, somebody who has the organization and the resources so they can get it before a lot more people than just the legislators."

"Hon," Bill said, "that's a big part of my job. But you watermen still need to be involved. Since you are the first to be directly affected by problems in water quality, you need to speak out on issues like sewage treatment, and land runoff, and industrial discharge. Groups like ours will be glad to provide you with any help we can."

"Yeah," Hon said as he turned toward the bench to glue the picture frame together, "but while you environmentalists are busy at tryin' to make the Bay better for tomorrow, we watermen are busy at tryin' to make a livin' from it today."

Our son, Jamie, came to visit us on his first vacation after accepting an engineering job in California. We spent a few days at home in North Carolina, then we drove to Crisfield so he could see his grandparents and his cousins and, of course, Hon. We arrived after dark on a cold, blustery Thursday. We hustled into the house with our bags, then sat down beside the kerosene heater to warm our hands and catch up on events there. Margaret said that Hon had finally given in and had his foot operated on. He was getting around some with a crutch, but he would not be able to work on the boat again until spring. He had been named Maryland's waterman of the month and also had been featured in the *Waterman's Gazette* for his efforts on behalf of the Chesapeake watermen, but neither of those had brought in any money. The picture framing and the Johns Hopkins project were keeping him going.

I was tired and the wind was bitter cold, so I decided against walking across the road to see him. When I awoke in the morning, I went right to the window and looked across the yard to see if his truck was in the driveway. It was not. I knew he would be having breakfast with his friends at the Circle Inn, so I climbed into my car and drove there to find him.

The little restaurant was almost empty. A couple of men were hunched over cups of coffee at the counter, the only other customers were Hon and Carroll Adams. I joined them at their table and ordered an omelette with orange marmalade for my toast. I told Carroll I still wanted to see the salt ponds behind his house, and asked when would be a convenient time. He said I could come that day. He had a few errands to run during the morning, but he would be home all afternoon.

"Bring some boots," he said. "We'll be tramping through the marsh to get there."

Hon couldn't go along because of his bad leg, but Jamie was interested, so right after lunch we rode out to Carroll's house near the Pocomoke Sound. He led us across his soybean field and into the thick woods that rimmed his farm. We followed a deer trail until we came out on a point of land overlooking a marsh that stretched for miles. A tidal creek meandered before us along the edge of the woods, then swung out into the marsh and disappeared in the tall reeds.

The point of land where we stood was a high marsh, too far above sea level for the salt loving reeds to grow but not quite high enough for pine trees or blackberry bushes. Except for two dry ponds, it was covered by a thick growth of grass called salt meadow hay.

"Those are the salt ponds," Carroll said. "Follow me."

Jamie and I shuffled through the grass behind him until we came to the nearest pond.

"Look at how hard the bottom of this pond is," Carroll said as he scraped his boot across it. "This is solid clay, perfect to prevent the water from being absorbed into the ground. That means it would evaporate and leave a salt skim."

"Out there," he said as he pointed toward a heavily wooded island standing in the midst of the sea of marsh, "on that hammock is where the Indians lived. Piles of oyster shells are still scattered around where they had their village."

Carroll then pointed eastward toward another wooded hammock.

"And there is where the last Indian lived. In the name of progress, the settlers cleared the woods to grow their tobacco and shot all the wildlife, leaving the Indians with nothing to eat. So they called a council and they all decided to move farther inland, except for him. He said he had lived his whole life here, and his fathers before him had lived their lives here, so he would stay. He picked up oysters along the shore of the Pocomoke Sound and caught turtles and muskrats in the marsh, and lived alone in his little hut on that hammock until he became sick and died. The ones who moved inland were no better off, though. They had to keep moving to stay ahead of the settlers until, finally, there was no place left for them to go, and then they all vanished."

The long shadows of late afternoon stretched across Hon's front yard by the time Jamie and I returned from Carroll's farm.

"Want to go to the creek?" Hon asked. "I gotta look at the boat to make sure the pump's workin'. She's leakin' again, and it's a lot easier to check on her than to get her up after she sinks."

I followed behind him as he hobbled along with his crutch down the narrow wharf until he reached the boat. He didn't try to go aboard. I could see that every step he took was painful, so I offered to climb down into the boat and check the water level.

"Naw," he said, "it's ridin' high enough to show it's all right."

He stood there a long time, just looking at the boat. When he finally spoke, he was still facing it. He didn't seem to be talking to me.

"With my leg hurtin' the way it is," he said, "I'm goin' to be laid up ashore a long time. When I was out there with my tongs, the only thing I could think about was catchin' as many oysters as I could. Now, I wonder if there'll be any left for me next year.

"Much as I hate to admit it, the Department of Natural Resources is the only hope I have of ever catchin' another oyster. If we don't see a better spawn this year, and if they don't have a better survival rate, we're out of business. Just about any action the Tidewater Fisheries Division takes to improve either the spawn or the survival rate, though, is goin' to end up bein' a restriction on us watermen, and we'll fight it. Doesn't matter whether we win that fight or not, we'll lose out in the end, because whatever they do is certain to fail anyway unless the water quality improves, and they don't have the power to do anything about that. We've got to look somewhere else for help, 'cause we're not bein' killed by what's happenin' on the Bay. Our problems are comin' from what's happenin' on the land.

"That's the responsibility of the other divisions of the Department of Natural Resources, but they haven't been given either the authority or the muscle to do what needs to be done, and they aren't likely to in the near future, either, 'cause the people ashore are fightin' them just the way we've been fightin' the Tidewater Fisheries.

"Some day, when there's no ground water left fit to drink and the beaches are so saturated with toxins they're not safe to walk on, then people will be screamin' for the government to do somethin' about it, whatever the cost. But that's not goin' to happen soon enough to help me, so I might as well make my plans to stay ashore. Hate to do it, but my art business is pickin' up pretty good. People like pictures of ducks and geese and bugeyes and skipjacks, and most every one they buy from me I get to frame. I believe I can make enough money to get by, that's all I need."

He raised his head and stared toward the crimson ball of a winter sun that was sinking into the Bay. The entire western sky was ablaze, its reflection turning the water into a river of fire.

"Looks like this day has come to an end," he said as he leaned heavily on his crutch and looked down at the old boat.

"Tomorrow," he said, "ought to be a fine day for oysterin'."

And maybe, someday, it will. The choice is ours to make.

Postscript

The Chesapeake Bay is a huge laboratory, the site of a massive experiment to determine if people can continue to live along the shores of a desirable estuary without destroying the life within it. One conclusion has already become obvious. Without controls, they cannot.

In the state of Maryland, the Department of Natural Resources has been given the responsibility for protecting the Bay, which means they are the agency of the government that must control the people who live and work around it. At one time or another, almost every one of us will come to resent them because of that. We do not like for them to interfere with our supposedly God given rights to catch oysters, and kill ducks, and use our land as we choose, and save money by pouring our wastes into our rivers and streams.

Many regulations recommended by the Department of Natural Resources have been approved by the legislature, and a majority of the industries and sewage treatment plants in the Bay's watershed are conscientiously abiding by them. Others, however, continue to reap short term profits by ignoring necessary control practices, and the political power of certain groups has weakened some regulations with loopholes that allow offenders to legally continue avoiding their share of the responsibility. Therefore, restoration programs to date have failed to reverse declining water quality trends.

The watermen are the first to suffer, so this story is written from their point of view. There are other points of view, of course, and they will be defended by their proponents with the same vehemence that the watermen defend theirs.

After all arguments have been expressed, however, the fact will still remain that the marine life once so abundant in the Bay is rapidly disappearing and will never be able to replenish itself in spite of all our hatcheries and our restrictions on fishing, unless the water quality improves.

Those of us who are concerned about the deteriorating water quality can follow one of two courses of action. We can remain passive, allowing the claims and the pressures of the polluters to go uncontested, and watch conditions worsen to the point that we all begin to suffer along with the watermen, or we can become involved and join forces with other concerned citizens to bring the problems to light and force corrective action.

I have chosen to become involved. I have joined the Chesapeake Bay Foundation, a highly effective non-profit organization working to "Save the Bay." It has offices in Annapolis, Richmond, and Harrisburg. If you would also like to support this foundation's work, or to volunteer your time in their effort, I urge you to write to: Chesapeake Bay Foundation, 162 Prince George Street, Annapolis, Md. 21401. Or, you can call them at (301) 268-8816.

As for Crisfield, perhaps you would like to visit there, explore the town and the docks, stay overnight, enjoy one of the fine seafood restaurants, and take one or more of the cruises that leave the harbor every day. And, while you are there, you may want to look up Hon. He'll be happy to sell you a picture of a duck or a skipjack, and to tell you what the Bay could be like if we all became as serious about water quality as he is.

Or, if you are looking for an interesting speaker for your next club meeting, you might want to call Hon. His number is (301) 968-2756.

Acknowledgments

I need to thank a lot of people for helping me. I'm sure I will neglect to mention some, and I hope they will forgive me. The people who come to mind are:

- Woodrow Wilson, who saved and published the historical records of Crisfield.
- Dick Coman, who encouraged me in a lot of ways.
- Bob and A.J. Lippsom, and Bill Goldsborough, who helped simplify scientific findings.
- Sara Clatterbuck, Shirley Ennis, Elizabeth Hall, Dick and Susan Hutchins, Etta King, and Brad Kramer who read the manuscripts and offered advice.
- Bryan Blake, who shared his boat building knowledge.
- Elmer Riggin, Carroll Adams, Laura Ritter, and Max Chambers, who shared their experience.
- Mr. Minton, who shared his genealogical information.
- Ed 'The Editor' Cottingham, who made me rewrite every paragraph.
- Fred Brown, who set the type and caught a surprising number of my typos in the final edit.
- Virginia, whose patience allowed me to work the long hours.
- Hon, whose love for the Bay made the book possible.

Bibliography

Brewington, H. V. *Chesapeake Bay Log Canoes and Bugeyes*, Cambridge, Md., 1963.

Burgess, Robert. *This Was Chesapeake Bay*, Cambridge, Md., 1963.

———, *Chesapeake Circle*, Cambridge, Md., 1965.

Chowning, Larry S. *Bearcat Skipper*, Centerville, Md., 1983.

Kennedy, Victor S., and Linda L. Breisch. "Sixteen Decades of Political Management of the Oyster Fishery in Maryland's Chesapeake Bay," *Journal of Environmental Management*, Volume 16, 1983.

Shomette, Donald G. *Pirates of the Chesapeake*, Centerville, Md., 1985.

Simpkins, Lloyd L. *Somerset County 1500 - 1700*, Princess Anne, Md., 1985.

Tawes, William I. *God, Man, Saltwater, and the Eastern Shore*, Cambridge, Md., 1977.

Tilp, Fredrick. *The Chesapeake Bay of Yore*, Alexandria, Va., 1982.

Wallace, Adam. *Parson of the Islands*, Cambridge, Md., 1961.

Warner, William W. *Beautiful Swimmers*, Boston, 1976.

Wennersten, John R. *The Oyster Wars of Chesapeake Bay*, Centerville, Md., 1981.

Wharton, James. *The Bounty of the Chesapeake*, Williamsburg, Va., 1957.

Wilson, Woodrow T. *History of Crisfield and Surrounding Areas of Maryland's Eastern Shore*, Baltimore, 1973.

———, *Thirty-Four Families of Old Somerset County, Maryland*, Baltimore, 1974.

———, *Crisfield Maryland, 1676-1976*, Baltimore, 1977.

Glossary

brogan - a large log canoe with a cabin.

bugeye - a very large log canoe decked over like a schooner, later versions made from planks rather than carved from logs.

crab pot - a cube-shaped crab trap made from galvanized wire and attached to a bouy.

crab scrape - a metal frame with a net dragged behind a boat to scoop crabs off the bottom.

drudging - scraping oysters off the bottom by dragging a heavy frame with iron teeth and a chain link net.

float - (noun) a crab pen, made of cedar slats, that floats half-sunken in protected waters.

log canoe - a boat carved from a log, or from several logs that are fastened together.

mananose - (pronounced man'ose) thin shelled clam; Algonquin word meaning 'to pick up'.

shedding - the process of holding crabs in floats or tanks until they discard their hard shells and become soft crabs.

shucking - opening oysters or clams by inserting a thin knife blade between the shells and cutting the muscle that holds the shells together.

skiffing gun - a huge, muzzle-loading shotgun that hunters laid upon the deck of a skiff to fire.

skipjack - a shallow draft plank boat, smaller version for crabbing and larger version for oyster drudging.

soft crab - a freshly molted, extremely defenseless and especially delicious crab.

spat - a very small oyster that has recently attached to a hard surface.

Index

Ordering Information

This book may not be available at book dealers in all parts of the country. If you cannot find it in your area, send $10.45 to the following address and the book will be mailed to you fourth class. For speedier delivery by first class mail, add $1.50.

Crisfield Publishing Company
Rt. 1, Box 295
Crisfield, MD 21817

Of course, the price of the book is subject to change without notice. In the event of a price change, you will be billed for the difference.